D0934003

Twayne's United States Authors Series

EDITOR OF THIS VOLUME

David J. Nordloh
Indiana University

Ignatius Donnelly

TUSAS 362

IGNATIUS DONNELLY

By DAVID D. ANDERSON
Michigan State University

TWAYNE PUBLISHERS
A DIVISION OF G. K. HALL & CO., BOSTON

Copyright © 1980 by G. K. Hall & Co.

Published in 1980 by Twayne Publishers,
A Division of G. K. Hall & Co.
All Rights Reserved

Printed on permanent/durable acid-free paper and bound
in the United States of America

First Printing

Frontispiece photo of Ignatius Donnelly © by John Collier, England,
Courtesy of The Collections of the Minnesota Historical Society

Library of Congress Cataloging in Publication Data

Anderson, David D.
Ignatius Donnelly.

(Twayne's United States authors series; TUSAS 362)
Bibliography: p. 122–25
Includes Index.
1. Donnelly, Ignatius, 1831–1901–
—Criticism and interpretation.
PS1545.D55Z53   818'.409   79–27600
ISBN 0–8057–7303–7

To my mother,
Nora M. Anderson

Contents

About the Author

David D. Anderson's long interest in American literary and intellectual history and criticism has produced sixteen books, including five for Twayne, *Louis Bromfield* (TUSAS), *Brand Whitlock* (TUSAS), *Abraham Lincoln* (TUSAS), *Robert Ingersoll* (TUSAS), *Woodrow Wilson* (TWLS), and hundreds of articles, essays, and short stories in the *Yale Review*, *Mark Twain Journal*, the *Personalist*, and many other journals. He is currently editor of the *University College Quarterly* and *MidAmerica*, the yearbook of the Society for the Study of Midwestern Literature, which he founded in 1971.

Recipient of many awards, including the Distinguished Faculty Award from Michigan State University, where he is Professor of American Thought and Language, and the Distinguished Alumnus Award from Bowling Green State University, he was Fulbright Professor of American Literature at the University of Karachi, Pakistan, and he has lectured throughout Europe, Asia, and Australia. He is currently at work on *William Jennings Bryan* for Twayne, a photo biography of Sherwood Anderson, and a cultural history of the Midwest.

Preface

In the past decade, Ignatius Donnelly has attracted a good deal of attention from historians and critics, attention that now matches that given Donnelly for many years by those who, for one reason or another, have been attracted to the myth of Atlantis, the subject of his first book. More recently, Donnelly has been discovered by literary scholars, who have begun to examine his career as a man of letters.

The reasons for all this continued and new attention are as varied as Donnelly himself. His political career paralleled the history of radical and reform politics from the antislavery 1850s to the campaigns against power and privilege nearly half a century later; his literary career in many ways anticipated that of the writer–reformer–political-activist work of Clarence Darrow and Brand Whitlock at the same time that it united the utopian vision of his contemporaries, particularly Edward Bellamy, and the realistic-naturalistic vision of Stephen Crane and Theodore Dreiser. As a scientific theorist, Donnelly revitalized the Atlantean myth defined by Plato, and he gave it an aura of respectability for generations whose search for meaning has demanded scientific verification and support.

All this, the range and breadth of a man at once a creature of his time and the creator of many of its myths as well as its social values, has, for nearly three generations after Donnelly's death, combined to make him a figure more mythical than real, more attractive for the bizarre qualities of his careers than for the impressive list of his accomplishments, for his failures as much as his successes.

Consequently, the attempt to examine Donnelly with objectivity, to understand his work, and to place him in historical perspective has been long overdue, and the work of the present generation of scholars is indeed welcome for the insights it gives not only into Donnelly's life and work but also into the age of which he was so vital a part. Still, though much effort has been made in the past twenty years to understand and assess Donnelly and his work, more remains to be done.

Scholarly study of Donnelly needs to concentrate on two aims in particular: to dispel the preoccupation with the bizarre in his works by examining the function and significance that lie beyond it, and to examine his works as the pragmatic attempts at intellectual conversion Donnelly intended them to be. That conversion constitutes the ultimate unity of Donnelly's thought; invariably overlooked, it must be the point of departure in any analysis of Donnelly's contribution to and ultimate place in the American literature of his time as well as in the grand sweep of literary history from the beginning of the nation to our own time. It is also important to stress, in any examination of Donnelly's literary career, that he neither aspired to nor sought literary greatness; rather, there is a good deal of evidence to suggest that he regarded writing first of all for its pragmatic worth as a conveyor of ideas and a means of persuasion, and secondly as an escape from the demands of political warfare.

It is also important to examine and acknowledge the substance of his works: scientific syntheses; utopian and antiutopian speculation; an insistence upon the role of cataclysm as well as evolution in human and natural history; the conviction, in eighteenth-century fashion, that for every mystery in nature there is also, somewhere in nature, its solution; his conviction to the very end that Mind rather than mindlessness is the controlling force in the universe, and that man must emulate this Mind in his relations with other human beings and in the institutions he creates.

But of most importance in any study of Ignatius Donnelly as a writer is recognition of the nature of Donnelly the man, writer of the works that bear his name. As the study of his works clearly shows, Donnelly was not the cultist some insist that he was; he was also not the imperialist, the racist, the authoritarian, the bigot, the demagogue that some critics insist that his works show him to be.

Nor, it is important to note, was Donnelly the shining knight dedicated to the defense of mankind against the assaults of those who would enslave him, the dispenser of justice, the champion of democracy, the demander of equality. This, too, is a mythological Donnelly, an image that contains much of reality in its portrayal but which at the same time ignores much else. It omits all that made him a human influence, largely for the good, in the affairs of Minnesota and the nation during the half-century that saw America reject one kind of human slavery and flirt with another as it transformed itself from an agricultural society to an industrial force.

Perhaps nowhere in American literary history can one find a writer whose works mirror more clearly what he believed about the nature of man and the universe, and the relationship, ideal and real, between man and the society he has created. Because Donnelly wrote as rapidly as he thought, because no abstract standard of literary art forced him to make his writing conform to something outside himself, because there is little evidence of serious attempts at revision in his existing manuscripts, it is evident that the relationship between Donnelly's thinking and convictions and what he wrote is as complete as it is possible to find anywhere in American literary history.

Recognition of that relationship is necessary in any serious attempt to assess Donnelly's achievement as a writer, and it is the controlling principle in this study. Nevertheless, I am not attempting to write a biographical study, but, insofar as the distinction is possible, a critical biography in which those biographical elements that shed light on Donnelly's development, purpose, and accomplishment as a writer are included. Biographical elements that do not serve that purpose, regardless of their interest or appeal, are minimized or excluded. At the same time, I focus my attention on the works themselves in order to determine what they say, the effectiveness with which they speak, and the place that they—and their creator—must occupy in the literary history of the nation. Donnelly was not a serious literary artist, but neither did he pretend to be, and his ultimate place can only be minor. Nevertheless, he wrote with conviction and power, and he expressed some of the most compelling, intriguing ideas in his day and ours. He is deserving of our serious attention. The result of such attention here, I hope, will be at once a serious evaluation of a serious writer of serious, often profound works, and a tribute to a curious, compassionate, determined, and ambitious man who was one of the most complex of his age.

DAVID D. ANDERSON

Lansing, Michigan
Ripshin Farm, Troutdale, Virginia

Acknowledgments

For the many kinds of assistance that enabled me to write this book, I am deeply grateful to the staffs of the Michigan State University Library; the State Library of Michigan, especially to Francis Scannell; and the Minnesota Historical Society; to friends and colleagues, especially Bernard F. Engel, Russel B. Nye, Ben Strandness, William Thomas, and William McCann for stimulation and comments; to Martin Ridge, as all scholars of Donnelly's life and work must be; to Toni Pienkowski for her efficient typing; and as always to Pat for so many things.

I am also indebted to the Minnesota Historical Society for permission to quote from the Donnelly Papers and for the use of the photograph of Donnelly used as the frontispiece of this volume, to the University of Chicago Press for their courtesy, and to Macmillan & Co. for permission to quote from David Kahn, *The Codebreakers* (New York: Macmillan & Co., 1967).

Chronology

1831   Ignatius Loyola Donnelly born in Philadelphia on November 3, the son of Dr. Philip Donnelly and Catherine Gavin Donnelly.

1837–   Educated in the public schools of Philadelphia; wrote poetry
1849   and kept notebooks. Graduates from Central High School.

1849–   Reads law as a clerk in the law office of Benjamin Harris
1852   Brewster. Becomes politically active as a Democrat.

1850   *The Mourner's Vision.*

1852   December 15: publicly criticizes Horace Greeley from a phrenology viewpoint.

1855   July 4: speaks on immigration at Democratic County Assembly in Independence Square. Selected by Democratic party as candidate for the state legislature; withdraws the day before the election and supports the Whig candidate. September: marries Kate McCaffrey.

1856   Supports the national Democratic ticket of Buchanan and Breckinridge. Becomes active in cooperative building associations. Unfairly accused of fraud. Decides to move West, visits Ohio, then settles in St. Paul, Minnesota, a frontier city. Begins to speculate in real estate. Forms partnership with John Nininger. By December begins to write and publish a newspaper, the *Emigrant Aid Journal.* Establishes and moves to Nininger City.

1857   Establishes the "Emigrant Aid Society." In the panic of August, loses his paper fortune. Starts the Dakota County Agricultural Society. Becomes an antislavery Democrat.

1858   Returns to practicing law. Becomes a Republican activist and organizer. Lectures on nonpolitical topics and on emigration to Minnesota. Endorsed as Republican candidate for state senate but defeated in November. Moves to St. Paul.

1859   Begins statewide letter campaign to secure nomination for statewide office; builds a strong Republican organization. Nominated for lieutenant governor. Writes the party's statement to the electorate. Elected lieutenant governor in November.

1859– Reads widely in political theory; lectures on education for
1861   farmers; serves as acting governor; attacks Stephen Douglas;
       debates the Democrats; supports the Union cause as secession
       begins. Charged with mobilizing the state for war; unsuccess-
       fully seeks appointment as colonel of volunteers. Renomi-
       nated for lieutenant governor; reelected in November.

1862   July 4. major speech on "War and Patriotism," opening
       campaign for Congress; nominated. Becomes liaison officer
       during Sioux uprising. Elected on "absolute equality" plat-
       form.

1863– Serves three terms as Republican in United States House of
1869   Representatives. Fails to secure renomination for fourth term.
       Supports the war, Reconstruction, railroad construction.
       Supports Lincoln strongly, although as a Radical he opposes
       Lincoln's Reconstruction policy; gradually breaks with Rad-
       icals.

1869– Becomes, successively, Liberal Republican, Granger, Green-
1879   back Democrat. Serves in state senate, 1875–78. 1874–79:
       edits *Anti-Monopolist*. 1878: defeated for Congress.

1880   Supports Democratic national ticket.

1882   *Atlantis: The Antediluvian World.*

1883   *Ragnarok: The Age of Fire and Gravel.*

1884   Runs unsuccessfully for Congress as Farmers' Alliance candi-
       date.

1887   Elected to state legislature as Farmers' Alliance candidate.
       The Great Cryptogram.

1888   Visits England.

1890   *Caesar's Column: A Story of the Twentieth Century.*

1891   *Doctor Huguet.*

1892   As Populist, writes preamble to the Omaha Platform. *The
       Golden Bottle.* Runs unsuccessfully for governor.

1893– Edits and publishes the *St. Paul Representative.*
1901

1896   Supports Bryan for the presidency. *The American People's
       Money.*

1899   *The Cipher in the Plays and on the Tombstone* privately pub-
       lished in March.

1900   Populist party candidate for the vice presidency.

1901   Dies shortly after midnight, January 1.

CHAPTER 1

Beginnings

IGNATIUS Loyola Donnelly was born at the beginning of a decade that was perhaps more influential in the development of the nation than any since the first decade of post-Revolutionary independence a half-century earlier: the decade of the 1830s. If during the fifty years between 1781 and 1831 the country had largely been attempting to find the means by which revolutionary rhetoric might become a workable political system, in the decade of the 1830s it had begun to find the means by which revolutionary ideology might provide the controlling philosophy for that system and make the promise of the eighteenth century a reality in the nineteenth.

Most intimately involved with the intellectual and ideological movements of that decade are two men and two loosely knit ideological movements. The men are Andrew Jackson, seventh president of the United States, and Ralph Waldo Emerson, the resident philosopher of Concord, Massachusetts, and the nation; and the movements are Jacksonian Democracy and romantic reform. From the beginning the movements were tied intrinsically to the men, but they are also so closely related to each other that they are different dimensions of a single movement best characterized, perhaps, by the nature of the age itself.

During that decade the promise inherent in the Declaration of Independence had begun to become reality; the promise of equality had begun to manifest itself in the rise of the common man, the individual, and the open society; and the promise inherent in the declaration of natural rights had begun to be reflected in an increasing demand for reform. All of this combined to produce first of all a faith in the perfectibility of man and his institutions, and secondly, the determination that both should be made perfect.

This faith and the determination that it engendered produced a good deal of dynamic action on almost every level of life in the Republic: the continued restless movement westward, with its concurrent growth of political strength; efforts to improve conditions for the poor, helpless, and imprisoned; the almost simultaneous

15

acceleration of activity in the temperance, women's rights, and abolition movements; desperate political warfare designed to capture more power for the people and their agents in government; and, on the highest philosophical level, the practical political level, and the evangelical religious level, the ennobling of the individual.

This decade was also responsible for a good deal of the American reputation for inventiveness, for practicality, and for a reverence for progress as suggested by numbers: technical innovation in travel ranged from the introduction of horse cars in New York City to railroad travel from Baltimore to Washington and beyond and steam packet travel on the trans-Atlantic run; Cyrus McCormick's reapers began to make possible the establishment of prairie farms; and the typecasting machine began what was eventually to become a flood of information. Between the census of 1830 and that of 1840 the population of the country increased by one-third, about five million people, and states as diverse as Michigan and Arkansas were added to the Union. Forces unleashed by a determined people, fueled by the revolutionary ideology of the past, had begun to reshape the nation into something truly unique in the history of nations.

I Early Writing

Born in Philadelphia on November 3, 1831, and destined to be shaped by those forces and, in turn, to contribute to their strength, Ignatius Loyola Donnelly was the son of an Irish immigrant, Dr. Philip Donnelly, who had become a physician in America, and his wife, Catherine Gavin Donnelly, of Irish ancestry, of a family who had thoroughly absorbed the values of their Quaker neighbors during their two generations in America.[1] Thus, while Philip Donnelly studied at the Philadelphia College of Medicine after their marriage, Catherine established a pawn shop to provide for their growing family, and, although Philip died of typhus only two years after beginning to practice, the lesson of both parents was clear to the son: one might rise in the world through his own efforts, if he were willing to do whatever was necessary, in spite of hardships.

The early loss of their father seemed to have had little effect on the Donnelly children. Like their father, they determined to rise by taking advantage of the educational opportunities that Philadelphia offered, particularly the public schools, which were then, largely because of the efforts of Dr. Benjamin Rush, among the best in the nation. Young Ignatius attended the Ringgold Grammar School, in Moyamensing's Third Ward, on the edge of the city.

Donnelly's high-school years at Philadelphia's Central High School, from which he graduated in 1849, were particularly important. Not only did they mark a major step forward in America's open society—a step taken by only a few of Donnelly's contemporaries—but Central High School, under the direction of Alexander D. Bache, and, after Bache became President of Girard College, his successor, John S. Hart, had a curriculum comparable to many American colleges at the time. While new radical colleges such as Oberlin (founded 1833) stressed "Learning and Labor," Central stressed mathematics, chemistry, physics, literature, and the classical languages as well as modern French. The curriculum was designed to produce leaders, natural aristocrats, in the new society. That many of his classmates were also artificial aristocrats could scarcely have escaped the observant young Donnelly.

Particularly influential upon Donnelly was Headmaster Hart, "the most aristocratic individual in this country, not excepting the President of the United States,"[2] who imbued Donnelly with his own love of the English classics and respect for the language. Of the classics, Hart constantly reiterated, as Donnelly recounted in his English lesson book, "Chaucer, Spencer, Shakespeare, and Milton are the four great landmarks in English literature. . . . They are the Gods of our language, the deities of the English language."[3] Interestingly, Hart did not cite Bacon as a master, although Donnelly was to become his champion in the authorship controversy. However, Hart recognized Donnelly's talent for language and his propensity for hard work.

Under Hart's instruction and encouragement, Donnelly read widely in the English classics, both prose and poetry, and began to develop his own style, briefly editing and writing for a student newspaper, the *Minute Book*, of which one copy survives. In the surviving copy, Donnelly included a sonnet of his own called "Life." As sophomorically profound as one might expect, its form is faithfully Shakespearean.

At least as important in introducing Donnelly to the power and beauty of language was the role of the school and its headmaster in applying the diligent work habits he had brought with him to the mastery of its use. Of a number of poems written during his high-school years, "The Mourner's Vision," published in 1850, a year after graduation, is by far the most important, both for the obvious determination with which Donnelly emulated his English masters and for the emotional and intellectual position from which it attacks the antiliberal forces of Europe and supports the growing American sentiments of nationalistic democracy. Mournfully yet powerfully he begins:

> Alas! a nation's wrecked hopes, and the might
>   That stirred the strong right arm for that nation's sake;
> Alas! the brave ones striving for the Right
>   Who bade that Lazarus of Truth awake;
>   All, all were following in that banner's wake;
> And all went down before the dastard blow,
>   When Russian lightnings bade the broad night quake,
>   And left me friendless in my grief below,
> To grope alone through memory's valley I waste of woe.

From regret, Donnelly moves quickly to defiance:

> Oh! Austria the vile, and France the weak,
>   My curse be on ye like an autumn storm,
> Dragging out tear drops on the pale year's cheek,
>   Adding fresh baseness to the twisting worm;
>   My curse be on ye like a mother's, warm,
> Red reeking with my dripping sin and shame;
>   May all my grief back-turned to ye, deform
> Your very broken image, and a name
> Be left ye which Hell's friends shall hiss and curse the same.[4]

Though the poem is weak in execution, perhaps suggesting an attitude toward form that was to manifest itself in his novels forty years later, or more likely reflecting the Emersonian dictum that form follows idea, it reflects very strongly the liberal American attitude toward the European liberal revolutions of 1848 and their suppression, and it marks the beginning of Donnelly's sympathy for the oppressed. It illustrates, too, the beginning of Donnelly's lifelong interest in writing verses while only rarely consenting to their publication.

The reason for this reluctance may have been Donnelly's concern, expressed in the preface to "The Mourner's Vision," that his friends not remind him of his foolishness in publishing the poem. But in spite of shyness real or alleged, Donnelly sent a copy of the poem to Oliver Wendell Holmes, a gesture that brought a long reply from the Master, with criticism as appropriate as it was sensitive:

I will give you then a little of the advice which you have courted, with a free tongue but kind spirit. You have the inward adjustments which naturally produce melody of expression and incline you to rhythmical forms, of which you will easily become a master. You are a bright scholar, who has read a good many books and perhaps have a little too much fondness of ornamenting your own composition with phrases borrowed from what you have read . . . a little too freely interspersed. You have a quick eye and a smart wit of your own—dangerous gifts, which like young colts must be bitted and broken before they can become trusted servants. Whether you have the higher requisites which make up the true poetical character or not, I dare not undertake to decide on the strength of a school exercise. . . .

. . . Be patient—do not listen to partial friends,—choose subjects worthy of sincere effort, whether grave or gay,—subdue the rank luxuriance of your infancy and language by studying the pure models and by and by we shall hear of Ignatius L. Donnelly.[5]

As sound as was Holmes's advice, Donnelly nevertheless continued to write and submit poems to popular journals for possible publication. In April 1852 he published in *Graham's Magazine* "The Forest Fountain," with a technique more improved if still derivative, and with more conventional subject matter than "The Mourner's Vision" but with a vividness of imagery and metaphor that justified Holmes's observation that he had a keen eye. In conventional, careful couplets, he wrote of sunset in the forest, of bright flames fading in the dusk, of blue sky reflected in a darkening pool, and of strange voices in the silence:

> And I hear, though indistinctly, voices of the
>   lost and gone:
> His whose bark went down in tempest; his whose
>   life and death were gloom;
> His whose hopes and young ambitions fell and
>   faded on the tomb;
> Oh, again his earnest language breaks upon my
>   dreaming ear,
> And I catch the tones that waking, I shall
>   never, never hear.[6]

II *Beginning a Career*

Although his interest in writing poetry remained strong during the early years of the 1850s, it was perhaps inevitable that Donnelly was attracted to the practice of law as a career and to political activism in the Democratic party. Again taking advantage of the open society in mid-nineteenth century America, as like his father he sought membership in a respected profession, he began in 1849 to read law as a clerk in the office of Benjamin Harris Brewster. A member of a wealthy New Jersey family and a leading Philadelphia lawyer, Brewster was destined to become Attorney General of Pennsylvania and then of the United States.

Donnelly was apparently uncomfortable in the staid, fashionable atmosphere of the lawyer's office, particularly because of coolness between Donnelly and his two fellow students, both of them apparently of backgrounds like that of their mentor. After three years, feeling capable enough to practice law on his own, Donnelly resigned, writing Brewster that

... the one became boorish and overbearing, the other distant and cold. I lived with them, as it were, *per gratia*. The bond of connection has never been a pleasant one,—and I sever it without regret—but for yourself, accept, sir, my reiterated apology for that in which I have offended you, and believe me when I say, that the honor of that intimacy you were pleased to extend to me shall live with me as one of the proudest memories; that your counsels and your precepts shall come before me in after years and that if accident of fortune can be waived aside from the path of any man, the day will come when some small part of the pride I see in my tutor will be returned to him by his student.[7]

As he left his legal apprenticeship, Donnelly at twenty-one became active in Philadelphia's Democratic party, beginning an allegiance that was to last little more than five years. But just as it was inevitable that in the early years of the 1850s Donnelly would become a Democrat, it was equally inevitable that he would become a member of the new Republican party before the decade was over.

Not only was the Democratic party of the 1830s and 1840s the party of Jacksonian Democracy, but it was also the party of the immigrants, largely German and Irish, who had fled the tragic vicissitudes in their homelands—famine, revolution, and oppression—only to find nativism and Know-Nothingism in America. During Donnelly's youth, Philadelphia itself was wracked by bigotry, prejudice, and even riots. Perhaps some of the bad feeling between Donnelly and his fellow law clerks had come from that hostility. The Democratic party, for those who felt the results of nativism, had become the party of the immigrant as well as of the common man.

Concurrently, by 1852 both John C. Calhoun and Daniel Webster had made their great declarations of principles in the Senate—the former sectional and the latter national; Henry Clay had made his last great compromise; California had become a free state; the new Fugitive Slave legislation had appeared on the nation's statute books;

and the three great leaders had passed on, leaving behind a nation apparently peaceful in spite of the echoes from Boston, from Oberlin, from Charleston, and the new, strange-sounding names of Kansas and Nebraska. To Donnelly in 1852 the Democratic party was the party of the people, and he was one of them.

One of Donnelly's first pieces of political writing, the text of a speech delivered in Philadelphia on December 15, 1852, was also indicative of his interest in the pseudoscience of his age, an interest that was to culminate in *Atlantis* (1882), *Ragnarok* (1883), and the substance of much of his later fiction. In otherwise undistinguished prose, he interpreted—not inaccurately—the relationship between the shape of Horace Greeley's head and the nature of his thinking. Greeley's championship of fads and causes ranging from socialism to a high tariff could, to Donnelly, be best explained in phrenologic terms: Greeley's head possessed, he wrote,

The characteristics common to the heads of visionary, theoretical reformers: that of largeness, fulness or overplus of brains with the front deficient in the development of those organs of judgement necessary to restrain and direct the active forces of the general intellect;—leaving to the mind its activity, its ambition, its perception, but depriving it of its practicality and its clear every day view of an every day world.[8]

Donnelly and Greeley were later to make a temporary political truce and alliance (and Donnelly might, certainly unaware, have been describing himself, as later photographs suggest). But Donnelly gained in local Democratic prominence even while his law practice remained unsuccessful and essentially trivial. The featured speaker for the county Democratic party assembled in Independence Square on July 4, 1855, Donnelly spoke strongly on the role of America in accepting and assimilating the poor and helpless from Europe. In an atmosphere permeated by Know-Nothingism, the speech was as unequivocal as it was courageous.

Donnelly supported the national Democratic ticket of James Buchanan and John Breckinridge in 1856, although the year before he had withdrawn from candidacy for the state legislature and supported his opponent, a Whig strongly opposed to the Know-Nothings. Already there seemed to be an element of ambiguity in his political allegiances. In 1858 he cast his first Republican ballot.

However, there was little if any ambiguity in his religious position. Although his mother and five sisters remained devout Catholics—his younger sister, Cecilia Eleanor Donnelly (1838–1917)

became a poet well known for her devotional verse—Donnelly dropped his Catholicism together with his middle name and remained largely aloof from organized religion for the rest of his life—never interfering, however, with the religious practice of his two wives, Kate, the first, whom he married in 1855, a Catholic, and Marion, the second, a Methodist. Religion apparently was to Donnelly the province of women, although later, in *Doctor Huguet* (1891) and *The Golden Bottle* (1892), he made eloquent pleas for a return to traditional Christian brotherhood.

Although Donnelly's mother and his wife Kate were both devout Roman Catholics, neither woman would tolerate the other, apparently because of real or imagined differences in social standing—in fact, they did not speak to each other for fifteen years. Donnelly's attitude ranged from amusement to disgust, commenting in his diary that the "pawnbroker's shop and the market stall [are] holding a heraldric [sic] disputation."

With this continued family dispute, an unsuccessful law practice, and increased family expenses, Donnelly began to look for means of supplementing his income. By 1856 he had become an officer in five cooperative associations, most of them devoted to building and financing homes for German and Irish immigrants. That same year, perhaps fleeing from a situation rapidly becoming difficult if not intolerable, he determined to move west. His decision, in the midst of continued negotiations by the societies, led to suspicions of fraud on his part, with a cousin, John Duross, insisting that Donnelly had made a large profit in reselling land to the Union Land and Homestead Building Association. Donnelly was cleared completely, but this experience, combined with a rumor that he had abused his trusteeship of funds willed his youngest sister, left Donnelly embittered. These rumors and others, all of them unsubstantiated and most of them disproved, followed Donnelly to the West, surfacing periodically for the benefit of political and personal enemies.

The convenience of emigration to the West was perhaps the most compelling reason for Donnelly's decision to leave Philadelphia, but there were undoubtedly others. In 1852 he had raised the possibility of a legal career in Chicago, and he had discussed moving west with Kate before their marriage, so it was evident that the idea was not new and that he did not see it as a means of escape.

Perhaps at least as significant as his personal position was the state of the country: by 1856 it was evident to all but the most imperceptive that the explosion was inevitable and that it was near. The record of the 1850s reads like the movement toward the denouement of a Greek tragedy: the compromise that compromised nothing in 1850; the Kansas-Nebraska dispute and bill in 1854; the disappearance of the Whigs and the emergence of the Republicans; the growing shadow of what was to become Dred Scott, Kansas, John Brown, and Harpers Ferry; and the emerging image of a rural Illinois lawyer named Lincoln. As Donnelly cast his vote for Buchanan and prepared to move west, he must have recognized the finality of both acts.

CHAPTER 2

Political Success and Failure in the West

I *The Frontier Developer*

WHEN Donnelly selected Minnesota as the locale of his new life, he did so by choice, having examined and rejected settlement in the older Midwest as being too settled and the newer West, Kansas, as too unsettled. At the same time he consciously left behind him a society relatively stable and closed, as well as his Catholic religion and his Democratic politics. All the evidence suggests that he also left behind whatever literary aspirations he may have had. His goal now was to build the country while he grew with it: he became a speculator and developer, in a booming territory that saw its population increase from 6,077 in 1850 to 172,023 and statehood in 1858.

Determined to ride the crest of that boom, Donnelly formed a partnership with John Nininger, also a former Philadelphian, who had established himself in St. Paul and had acquired substantial land holdings. Donnelly's talents, legal and promotional, were devoted to the enterprise, the first products of which were writing a good deal of promotional material for the partnership's newly established townsite, Nininger City, and establishing, editing, and writing the *Emigrant Aid Journal*, the first issue of which appeared in December 1856.

The *Emigrant Aid Journal*, the principal literary result of Donnelly's shortlived speculative career, was established simply for the promotion of Nininger City, as was the Emigrant Aid Society. But Donnelly envisioned the paper as becoming the leading paper of the West, just as he saw Nininger City becoming a river port, county seat, and eventually a great city. However, paper and city fell victim to the techniques of competitive speculation and the vagaries of economics, politics, and the times.

Donnelly's goal was made clear in the masthead of the paper: "'Dost thou know how to play the fiddle?' 'No,' answered Themistocles, 'but I understand the art of raising a little village into a great city.'" Donnelly was convinced that he shared that knowledge with Themistocles.

Circumstances—the economic recession of fall and winter 1857–58, the loss of the county seat of Dakota County to rival Hastings, personal difficulties with his partner and his brother, John Gavin Donnelly—combined, however, to limit and finally defeat Donnelly's efforts to build a great city. More frenzied efforts on his part revived old rumors and started new—he was, for example, rapidly gaining a reputation as "Ingeneous Doemly, with his city lots on paper selling for a thousand dollars each. . . ."[1]

Although more than a hundred houses had been built, plans begun for musical societies, a hotel discussed, and, early in 1858, the Dakota County Agricultural Society founded in Donnelly's home, his credit failed, and he returned to the practice of law while attempting to liquidate his land holdings before they were forfeited to the tax collector. By January 1858 it was evident that Donnelly's vision of himself as a city builder had become no more than a passing dream, in spite of his efforts. His failure, he was convinced, was good for his character.

II *The Young Politician*

Donnelly's return to the practice of law meant, simultaneously, a return to practical politics—not, however, the Democratic party of his past, but the new Republican party of the antislavery West. In September 1857 Donnelly had been elected secretary of the Republican Territorial Convention in St. Paul, and later that fall, after organizing the party in Dakota County in conjunction with his close friend Dr. Thomas Foster, he was nominated for the territorial senate. That fall, however, Dakota County went Democratic, although Donnelly lost by only three hundred votes.

Whether encouraged by the narrowness of his defeat or enjoying the exhilaration of political warfare after his abortive effort at city-building, or perhaps something of both, Donnelly was in politics—specific reform politics—to stay. When Foster went to St. Paul to edit the new Republican newspaper the *Minnesotan*, Donnelly became undisputed Republican leader in Dakota County as well as an editorial writer for that newspaper. In 1858 he was again nominated for the Senate and again defeated. Donnelly and the party could not finance a campaign, but Donnelly was determined to become part of the party's statewide leadership as its members began to regroup and reorganize for the coming presidential campaign.

From the beginning of his campaign in the fall of 1858 through that in 1880 Donnelly was never far from the political conflicts that centered upon the great issues of the day, and often he was in the thick of the fighting. Consequently, during that twenty-two years, almost all his writing and speaking was devoted to the political ends that he sought at the moment, and, as his political loyalties altered as he changed in his pursuit of a workable ideal, the specific objectives and often the specific enemies changed; but the tactics he employed remained the same.

As the battle lines for 1860 began to be drawn, Donnelly determined to capture the vote of the German, Irish, and other foreign immigrants pouring into Minnesota, those who, like Donnelly himself, had traditionally been drawn to the Democratic party and who were largely responsible for Democratic gains in Minnesota in 1856 and 1858. In a letter published in the *St. Paul Minnesotan* on July 18, 1858, he wrote:

Laboring men of the old world! You are many of you at the foot of the ladder which all mankind are compelled to climb; you are clambering the rungs which the overthrow of the old world's aristocratic nations has left open to you. Which party will help you up? That which stands committed to the South and slavery, that which would reduce and has reduced labor to the degradation of bondage, which presents to it no destiny but shame and humiliation? Or that party, which with no dark record in the past, with no principle but those which the Declaration of Independence has set forth, with Equality, Liberty, Humanity, for all men, strives by doing the unalterable justice to the black, to advance the dignity and promote the welfare of the white race.[2]

Like Lincoln's Cooper Union Address, this declaration avoids the rhetoric of abolitionism, but instead, in terms reminiscent of Lincoln's arguments against Senator Stephen Douglas the previous summer, insists that whatever is done for the black man, the slave, is in keeping with American tradition and white self-interest. Arguments like these recur in Donnelly's political rhetoric for the rest of his life, and they are often evident in *Caesar's Column* (1890), *Doctor Huguet* (1891), and *The Golden Bottle* (1892).

As in the later novels and in much of his political rhetoric, however, Donnelly found it impossible to maintain a clear distinction between fact and fiction, and like so many others he determined to make his point forcefully and persuasively. In this letter he went on to frighten his immigrant readers by obviously asserting that there was already in the South a substantial number of white slaves whose number was expanding, a point upon which he was quickly challenged by the Democratic *St. Paul Pioneer* and the *Democrat*. Here, as in his later novels, Donnelly was evidently a believer in the efficacy of shock, a factor which, when challenged or refuted, never seemed to bother him.

Selected as the party's candidate for lieutenant-governor in the fall elections—Donnelly would have preferred the nomination for Congress—he also emerged as the party spokesman, serving in many ways on the state level as Lincoln had been attempting to do on the national, that is, to forge a common identity and unifying principle for a party whose members ranged from economic conservatives to economic liberals, from Whigs to Democrats, from those who found slavery distasteful to those who despised it. To bring about a measure of unanimity among these diverse groups on the national level, Lincoln gave his Cooper Union Address on February 27, 1860; the previous fall, Donnelly had attempted to do the same thing in his "An Address to the People of Minnesota in Regard to the History, Principles, Aims and Objects of the Republican and Democratic Parties."

In its fifty pages the "address" was again an attempt not only to propagate the cause of the Republicans, particularly among farmers and newcomers to Minnesota, but also to give form and focus to a party still largely unformed and without a clear party philosophy. Donnelly's points of emphasis were not unlike Lincoln's the following year: opposition to slavery; the recognition of human equality; support for a free, uncorrupted franchise; and, of most importance to those for whom the address was intended, support for the Homestead Act.

As candidate for lieutenant-governor he was attacked because, as an Irishman of Catholic origins, he should have remained a Democrat. He tried to define the nature of his political philosophy and the cause of his change, two demands that were to recur in his political career as he found new alliances and allegiances. In the *St. Paul Minnesotan* of August 4, 1859, he wrote:

I did not join the Republican party for success alone. I could have found that among the Democrats, by whom I was honored by the offer of high office. I became a Republican upon sober, solemn, honest conviction. I saw two paths: one led along the line defined by the founders of the government; it was rough and stormy, but it pointed to the perpetuity of freedom and the safety of our institutions. The other lay before me broad and crowded and full of prosperity, but it went downward to darkness and ultimate disaster to the country. I chose the rough and stormy path. I proclaimed myself a Republican in the midst of the most Democratic county in our State.[3]

During the ensuing campaign, Donnelly, who took upon himself the responsibility of speaking for national Republican issues and principles, emerged as an energetic, skilled stump speaker, backwoods campaigner, and demagogic orator. He seemed to thrive on the discomforts of the campaign trail, much to the alarm of his wife. On election day the Democratic party, split as badly in Minnesota as it was nationally, was overwhelmingly defeated, and Donnelly at twenty-eight was elected lieutenant-governor of Minnesota on the eve of civil war. He determined to be a wise, liberal, human public servant.

III   *The Congressman*

Donnelly's career as Republican lieutenant-governor through two terms was marked by a good deal of sharpening of his oratorical and maneuvering skills, but upon the outbreak of war he sought unsuccessfully to gain an appointment as colonel of a Minnesota volunteer regiment. His enemies insisted that he was only interested in the $2,500 yearly salary.

Nevertheless, Donnelly was a staunch supporter of the war effort and the principles for which it was fought. When the Sioux uprising took place in Minnesota in the spring of 1862, Donnelly joined the troops sent to suppress it. He apparently saw little if any fighting, but sent a graphic description of the civilian retreat from New Ulm to the *St. Paul Press*. Published on August 28, 1862, it demonstrated his compassion for the victims of war:

Never, perhaps, was a more melancholy cortege seen in the world than the one which stretched along the road from New Ulm to Mankato. There were mothers there [who] wept over children slaughtered before their eyes; strong men who in a moment had been stripped of their worldly wealth, of home, of wife, and of family; who had escaped into the grass with the death shrieks of parents, brothers, and sisters, ringing in their ears. All bowed down by an overwhelming grief and by an anxiety which no words can describe, but which in two cases had produced *actual insanity*.[4]

Although Donnelly's brief campaign and his reporting were controversial, they contributed further to his statewide reputation, and he returned home to secure the Minnesota soldier vote for the

Republicans, and, not coincidentally, for his own candidacy for Congress. His election secure as Minnesota's fourth congressman, he became as eager to dominate national politics as he had the state level. He made his first speech in the House on February 27, 1864, advocating a federal immigration bureau. He concluded:

With nearly one billion [acres] of unsettled lands on one side of the Atlantic, and with many millions of poor oppressed people on the other, let them organize the exodus which needs must come, and build, if necessary, a bridge of gold across the chasm which divides them, that the chosen races of mankind may occupy the chosen lands of the world.[5]

This curious combination of Jeffersonianism, manifest destiny, and white supremacy did not produce Donnelly's most effective rhetorical device, as the *St. Paul Pioneer* was quick to point out, attributing to Lincoln the remark that "every member of Congress from the West for the last twenty years has been making the same speech." But others praised his mastery and presentation of facts. The ideology inherent in the speech was to return in other forms, primarily in Donnelly's novels, in later years.

His second speech, in September 1864, dealt with the Reconstruction issue, and it was considerably more effective. Donnelly pointed out that the challenges of making peace were greater and more difficult that those of making war, concluding with a plea for firm reconstruction of a nation rather than a group of states:

We who come, Mr. Speaker, from the Far West have not that deep and ingrained veneration for State power which is to be found among the inhabitants of some of the older states. We have found that State lines, State names, State organizations, are in most cases the veriest creatures of accident. To us there is no savor of antiquity about them. Our people move into a region of country and *make* the State. We feel ourselves the offshoots of the nation. We look to the nation for our protection.[6]

Well received by the Republicans—in the speech Donnelly described Lincoln as "a great man . . . not after the old models of the world, but with a homely and original greatness"—it was condemned at length by the Democrats, and scurrilous stories about Donnelly's treachery in Minnesota and dishonesty in Philadelphia were repeated widely. His chances for reelection in 1864 seemed slim.

But in spite of renewed assaults against his honesty and little support from the Republican press, Donnelly was reelected in 1864, as he was in 1866. In 1868, however, with the party split over

Donnelly's candidacy, the Democratic candidate won with 13,506 votes to Donnelly's 11,265 and the other Republican candidate's 8,595. Had the party not split, obviously Donnelly would have been reelected, and he might have remained a Republican. But politics deals with reality, and Donnelly, who had supported the impeachment of President Andrew Johnson, was nevertheless moving away from the increasingly conservative radical leadership in Congress. During his last term he stumped Minnesota for black suffrage and endorsed the Wade-Davis Manifesto—both of which acts alienated nonradicals in Minnesota—and he accepted gifts of stock for aiding the cause of the Lake Superior and Mississippi Railroad from his strategic position on the Committee on Public Lands. He also worked to advance the cause of other Minnesota railroads, particularly the Hastings, Dakota and Western; but his relationships with the railroads bothered him, and he finally severed his ties with them.

Another of his causes was support for the creation of a National Bureau of Education to advance the cause of the freed blacks, and he followed that enthusiasm with an attempt to support the planting of forests on the western plains, an effort that eventually had some success. During his last months in Congress he supported the Alaska Purchase bill, and then he determined to campaign for reelection while at the same time working for election to the Senate.

Defeated in both, Donnelly had to scurry to find a means of earning a living. He became a Washington lobbyist for several railroads, and then, because of continued bad publicity, took the post of Washington correspondent for the *St. Paul Dispatch*. In a series of weekly articles he became increasingly critical of the Republicans. On March 1, 1870, he wrote, "The Republican party of the nation must choose between the people and the capitalists. . . . *If they take the side of the latter they must not expect the former to sustain them.* A party cannot live upon the memory of the past." A clear rejection of the Republican tariff was indicative of an ideological break; even more important was his rejection of the manner and morals of what had become the Gilded Age as he described a real or imagined Washington reception:

A carpet extends from the curb to the door. You enter. Stairs, hall, rooms, are packed with moving, jostling, surging, struggling people. Here a lady expostulates with a gentleman immediately behind for standing on her train, while he, good man, assures her he is straddling it, and the man who has fastened her to the spot is several feet distant in the crowd! In one of the rooms near the door stand the host and hostess, smiling away . . . and mechanically shaking hands with everybody in the pump handle style. . . . But the great clatter, jangle and chatter goes on, a thousand interests, wishes, vanities, mingle together in one stupendous buzz and burr, while the mechanical host and hostess stand smiling away and working their pump handles, and the streams struggle in and out of the door. . . .[7]

Not only was Donnelly moving closer to political radicalism during this period, as Martin Ridge has pointed out,[8] but at the same time his lobbying activities for Jay Cooke and others, together with his observation of the Washington scene during one of its most corrupt as well as glittering ages, was giving him the substance of what would result in his novels two decades later.

IV   *The Search for a Political Party*

In 1870 Donnelly formulated a political cause that would, he was sure, give him the political support he needed if he were to return to Congress. His banner was opposition to the protective tariff, by which, he was convinced, western farmers were robbed for the benefit of eastern manufacturers. Rejected by both Republicans and Democrats, he sought nomination as an independent. The new self-styled People's party gave him its endorsement, and the Democrats reluctantly followed. But the farmers of Minnesota were receiving forty cents a bushel more for their wheat than they had a year earlier, and Donnelly could not convince them that they were being victimized. He was defeated by 2,600 votes out of 32,000 cast. The loss was attributed by his supporters to his losing the votes of Northern Pacific Construction Company laborers, who were employees of a political enemy.

Reluctant to seek employment as a lobbyist, Donnelly returned to his farms, and in 1871 turned to lecturing on Minnesota's Lyceum circuit. Refusing to pay commissions to agents, he prepared his own tour. His two topics were "Six Years in Washington" and "American Humorists." His philosophy of the lecture is curiously unlike what was to become his literary philosophy when he began to write fiction. In the manuscripts of his speeches he noted what a speaker should do:

Avoid those topics which may conflict with the political or sectarian views of our audience, for although our own sincerity may be undoubted, we have no right to call the world together to assault its convictions, while the occasion permits no opportunity of replay. Neither should the lecturer, except incidentally, attempt to instruct his audience; the task is a difficult one, and it may chance that many among his readers may know more of the matter than he does himself. But while he avoids didactical dryness on the one hand he should not rush into trifling frivolities on the other,—or he will underestimate the average intelligence of mankind, and lessen the public estimate of his own. He should strive to . . . teach without pedantry, to please without wearying, and to enliven without becoming himself ridiculous.[9]

During these months Donnelly began to associate himself with the anti-Grant faction in the Republican party which became the Liberal Republicans. As the political wars beckoned again and there appeared to be a place for him in them, he left lecturing for his first love. Nevertheless, he gained the reputation of a humorist for his successful lecture on American humorists, and he used some of the material for the next two decades. When his political fortunes flagged, he turned to lecturing for income and for the appreciation of the crowd that he missed from the campaign trail.

For the rest of the decade Donnelly's political fortunes varied, as he became increasingly radical in his economics. Although he campaigned strongly for Horace Greeley for President in 1872, Donnelly was not a candidate, and when Greeley's defeat ended that hope, Donnelly turned to organizing—and leading—the new Granger movement in Minnesota. In 1873 he was elected Anti-Monopolist state senator, and in 1874 he became the radical leader in the state senate, his programs focusing upon control of the lumbering, banking and insurance, and railroad interests. In 1874, frustrated, he founded his own newspaper, the *Anti-Monopolist.*

But in the fall of 1875 he lost his Granger support, and in 1876 he took his followers, now the Independent Anti-Monopoly party, into the Greenback camp. He was temporary chairman of the national Greenback convention in 1876, an anniversary date that Donnelly exploited with glee. But the party nominated eighty-five-year-old Peter Cooper and went down to defeat. It was Donnelly's fate, it was clear, to remain in the state senate, and his new coalition made impressive gains in Minnesota the next year. In 1878 he was nominated for Congress as a Democrat, the result of another alliance, but his defeat in the midst of scandalous charges and countercharges led him to conclude in his diary on November 3, 1880, after two futile years of pursuing the congressional post once more:

This is my 49th birthday, and a sad day it is. . . . All my hopes are gone, and the future settles down upon me dark and gloomy indeed. . . . My life has been a failure and a mistake. My hopes have so often come to naught that I cease to hope. . . . Well. All I can do is to face the music and take the damnable future as it comes.[10]

But on December 31 he noted that "we shall fight on," and indeed he did—but in a different campaign: he was already at work on the book that was to become *Atlantis.*

CHAPTER 3

The Search for Scientific Truth

W HEN Donnelly began *Atlantis* his political and personal for- tunes were at their lowest. Not only had he suffered a series of defeats as his political philosophy moved leftward, but his influence had decreased, and farming, although improving, was still not the source of sufficient economic or personal fulfillment for him. However, he had a good deal of intangible capital upon which he had not yet drawn heavily: his creative imagination, his intellectual curiosity, and his tenacious conviction that somewhere in the world of fact and reality he would find truth.

Donnelly's interest in the Atlantis myth had a variety of origins. All his life he read voraciously in scientific and pseudoscientific litera- ture, and his interest had been whetted by the publication of Jules Verne's *Twenty Thousand Leagues Under the Sea* in 1870. His own ability to forge syntheses out of masses of seemingly unrelated detail had been developed in the course of writing and giving hundreds of stump speeches in dozens of campaigns. In amassing the information for *Atlantis* he followed the same pragmatic, essentially uncritical approach, selecting and interpreting material as it suited his pur- poses, and writing at the same furious pace at which he campaigned.

Donnelly knew the end of his research just as, in his legal and political work, he knew the results that he wanted, and from the beginning he determined to prove conclusively to the most skeptical reader that his theories were correct. Thus, by mid-March of 1881 he had his manuscript completed; it was accepted by Harper and Brothers, and by July it was in page proofs. Enthusiastically he wrote in his diary that "I feel like a mother listening to the first cry of her first born." It was a new beginning.

I Atlantis: The Antediluvian World

One of the most ancient and most provocative myths, the existence of a long-lost continent or island called Atlantis is best known from Plato's two brief dialogues, *Timaeus* and *Critias*, which Donnelly

33

includes as the second chapter of Part I of the book, that part in which he establishes the evidential proof for the lost land's former existence. But, as Donnelly and his successors make clear, there is much evidence that suggests an origin for the myth in at least one work that is lost as completely and irretrievably as the land it describes. According to Proclus (A.D. 410–485) in his Commentary on Plato's *Timaeus*, the lost land was first described in Marcellus's lost *History of Ethiopia*. Proclus writes that Marcellus described how "the inhabitants of several islands in the Atlantic Ocean preserved a tradition from their ancestors of the prodigiously great island of Atlantis which was sacred to Poseidon and held domination over all the islands in the Atlantic for a long period."

Proclus gives no suggestion of Marcellus's sources, and, as Plato suggests, the transmission of the myth had been largely oral, passing from Solon, who learned of the myth in Egypt but was prevented from using it in his work, to Dropides, to the elder Critias, to Callaeschrus, to the younger Critias, and thence to Plato himself. Nevertheless, Plato is the earliest recorded source of the myth, and it was Plato's account that first fired Donnelly's imagination and then his curiosity as it suggested a single logical explanation for the diverse legends and natural phenomena that had intrigued him since his youth. The resulting book was a major success, Donnelly's first, and it made him an international figure, a seriously regarded scientific theorist, and a central figure in an Atlantis-centered cult that continues to the present.

Although Plato treats Atlantis in two phases—the first, in *Timaeus*, dealing with the physical existence of the island and the second, the unfinished *Critias*, with the ideal commonwealth of Atlantis—Donnelly, the reformer, is unconcerned with the latter; instead, with only a single reference to the foolishness of gold worship, he devotes himself to proving the existence of Atlantis as a reality that had given rise to the myth, and he insists that it had, in effect, been the source of human civilization before its destruction through a natural calamity and its passage from reality into legend.

The book is clearly and tightly organized, from the initial thirteen "distinct and novel propositions," which Donnelly sets out to prove, to his vision of a future in which not only are the questions of man's past answered but in which knowledge of the past provides keys to understanding the problems of the present and future. Donnelly begins by defining his propositions:

    1.   That there once existed in the Atlantic Ocean, opposite the mouth of the

Mediterranean Sea, a large island, the remnant of an Atlantic continent, and known to the ancient world as Atlantis.

2. That the description of the island given by Plato is not . . . fable, but verifiable history.

3. That Atlantis was the region where man first rose from a state of barbarianism to civilization.

4. That it became . . . a populous and mighty nation, from whose overflowings the shores of the Gulf of Mexico, the Mississippi River, the Amazon, the Pacific coast of South America, the Mediterranean, the west coast of Europe and Africa, the Baltic, the Black Sea, and the Caspian were populated by civilized nations.

5. That it was the true Antediluvian world . . . representing a universal memory of a great land, where early mankind dwelt for ages in peace and happiness.

6. That the gods and goddesses of the ancient Greeks, the Phoenicians, the Hindoos, and the Scandinavians were simply the kings, queens, and heroes of Atlantis; and the acts attributed to them in mythology are a confused recollection of real historical events.

7. That the mythology of Egypt and Peru represented the original religion of Atlantis, which was sun-worship.

8. That the eldest colony formed by the Atlanteans was probably in Egypt, whose civilization was a reproduction of the Atlantic island.

9. That the implements of the "Bronze Age" of Europe were derived from Atlantis. The Atlanteans were also the first manufacturers of iron.

10. That the Phoenician alphabet, parent of all the European alphabets, was derived from an Atlantis alphabet, which was also conveyed from Atlantis to the Mayas of Central America.

11. That Atlantis was the original seat of the Aryan or Indo-European family of nations, as well as of the Semitic peoples, and possibly also of the Turanian races.

12. That Atlantis perished in a terrible convulsion of nature, in which the whole island sunk into the ocean, with nearly all its inhabitants.

13. That a few persons escaped in ships and on rafts, and carried to the nations east and west the tidings of the appalling catastrophe, which has survived to our own time in the Flood and Deluge legends of the different nations of the old and new worlds.[1]

The propositions Donnelly set out in the work are so comprehensive, if established, that they promise to provide the answers to the major problems and speculative phenomena observed and described by natural philosophers of the eighteenth and nineteenth centuries, the philosophers who laid the foundations for modern sciences ranging from geology to anthropology. Donnelly's propositions reject any suggestion that the Atlantis story transmitted by Plato was, in the nineteenth-century sense, a myth because it was untrue, because it was contrary to the reality described in the Bible for traditionalists or by modern science for those less traditionally inclined. At the same time, the completeness with which those thirteen propositions attempt a synthesis of all the observations and speculations of the then newly emerging, vaguely defined sciences of archaeology, comparative anthropology, and ethnology also denies the possibility of a later, more contemporary definition of myth as sacred history, as foundation of social life or culture, as pattern for human behavior, or as mode of being. For Donnelly not only is the Atlantis story real, but it provides the reality that lies beyond whatever civilizations, cultures, or varied memories of a long-lost Golden Age, Deluge, or *Ragnarok* exist among men, regardless of time or place of existence.

The rest of the book, divided into five parts, is a compilation of data ranging from scientific evidence to rumor to sheerest speculation, each bit of which, as Donnelly sees it, fits into the massive mosaic that he is determined to construct. Nearly every assertion or bit of evidence is supported by illustrations, ranging from a geological profile of the Atlantic Ocean to drawings of mounds and artifacts of the Ohio and Indus Valleys, all of which are further tangible evidence to support his synthesis.

After defining the propositions that the book is to prove in the first chapter, Part I reprints all of Plato's story—or history, as Donnelly calls it—as, in effect, the factual story that the book is to prove, and then examines the evidence supporting Plato's story. Not only are there, in Donnelly's words, "no marvels; no myths; no tales of gods, gorgons, hobgoblins, or giants" (p. 22)—in other words, none of the trappings of the marvelous, the fantastic, or the gothic—but as in Prescott's *Conquest of Peru* (1847), a straightforward description of different, even remarkable, but nevertheless recognizably human people in a recognizably human environment; there is no "moral or political lesson in the guise of a fable," but instead "a straightforward, reasonable history of a people ruled over by their kings, living and progressing as other nations have lived and progressed since their day" (p. 23), a story repeated many times in human history.

More important, however, in this first part, is the physical evidence that Donnelly amasses to support Plato's story: the geologic structure of Plato's island and the present Azores, including the nature of the rock and the presence of hot springs; parallel references in Proclus, Aelian, Marcellus, and in Isaiah and Ezekiel in the Old Testament, all of which he asserts can best be understood in the light of Plato's history; factors indicating the possibility of such a catastrophic occurrence, using evidence from human as well as geologic history; the structure of the Atlantic sea floor, including the existence of a "great elevation," Dolphin's Ridge; the evidence of flora and fauna, living and fossilized—all of which suggest connections and contacts once possible but recorded nowhere in the seven thousand years of human history.

Much as in a legal brief, Donnelly has, in the first part, established both the propositions that he intends to prove and their logicality in the light of observable, recorded, trustworthy human experience. Certainly one less determined to establish truth beyond all reasonable doubt might, with good reason, have been content to stop at this point. But for Donnelly establishing the reasonableness of his propositions was not enough: he was determined to establish not only their validity but their accuracy beyond the most remote doubt. The rest of the book demonstrates not only the diligence and scope of his research but the nature of his persuasive skill, as he amasses indiscriminately and uncritically fact, legend, conjecture, and deter- mination, puts them together, always skillfully and often logically, and extracts from the result the conclusions that he had already defined in the propositions he had set out to prove.

Thus, Part II is an exercise in comparative mythology, as Donnelly examines deluge legends from the Bible and other oral and written, religious and secular traditions, pointing out the unmistakable parallels that have been observed by so many others for so many other different reasons. For Donnelly, however, there can be only one conclusion: they are all part of the history, dimly remembered and often badly transmitted, of the cataclysm recorded by Plato. One can only conclude, according to Donnelly, that—

> The people of Atlantis, having seen their country thus destroyed, section by section, and judging that their own time must inevitably come, must have lived under a great and perpetual terror, which will go far to explain the origin of primeval religion, and the hold which it took upon the minds of men; and this condition of things may furnish us a solution of the legends which have come down to us of their efforts to perpetuate their learning on pillars, and also an explanation of that other legend of the Tower of Babel, which . . . was common to both continents, and in which they sought to build a tower high enough to escape the Deluge. (pp. 127–28)

This conclusion leads Donnelly logically from an exercise in comparative mythology to one in comparative anthropology as, in Part III, he compares the civilizations of two worlds, that of the traditional European, African, and Asian cradles of civilization and that of pre-Columbian America. In this section he not only continues the evidence found in parallels—in this instance in architecture, in invention, and in technological development—but he insists that the entire foundation of civilized society from the remote past to the beginning of the modern era—for Donnelly approximately the beginning of the American era—was nothing more than the inheritance from Atlantis: *"In six thousand years,"* he asserts, *"the world made no advance on the civilization it received from Atlantis"* (p. 130). Furthermore, a continuum exists to the present:

Phoenicia, Egypt, Chaldea, India, Greece, and Rome passed the torch of civilization from one to the other; but in all that time they added nothing to the arts which existed at the earliest period of Egyptian history. In architecture, sculpture, painting, engraving, mining, metallurgy, navigation, pottery, glass-ware, the construction of canals, roads, and aqueducts, the arts of Phoenicia and Egypt extended, without material change or improvement, to a period but two or three hundred years ago. The present age has entered upon a new era; it has added a series of wonderful inventions to the Atlantean list; it has subjugated steam and electricity to the uses of man. And its work has but commenced: it will continue until it lifts man to a plane as much higher than the present as the present is above the barbaric condition; and in the future it will be said that between the birth of civilization in Atlantis and the new civilization there stretches a period of many thousands of years, during which mankind did not invent but simply perpetuated. (pp. 130–31)

Furthermore, Donnelly insists that arguments for the development of civilization in parallel patterns or in similar ways at different periods of time are simply untenable; in rejecting the implications of Darwinism applied to the development of social bodies as well as biological organisms, he asserts that the acquisition of civilized traits is not something that happens to a people in the course of their development, but is the result of innate ability present from the beginning:

Civilization is not communicable to all; many savage tribes are incapable of it. There are two great divisions of mankind, the civilized and the savage; and, as we shall show, every civilized race in the world has had something of civilization from the earliest ages; and as "all roads lead to Rome," so all the converging lines of civilization lead to Atlantis. The abyss between the civilized man and the savage is simply incalculable; it represents not alone a difference in arts and methods of life, but in the mental constitution, the instincts, and the predispositions of the soul. . . . This abyss . . . has never been passed by any nation through its own original force, and without external influences, during the Historic Period; those who were savages at the dawn of history are savages still. . . . Gauls, Goths, and Britons . . . were not savages, they possessed written languages, poetry, oratory, and history . . . religious ideas . . . weapons of iron. . . . The Roman civilization was simply a development and perfection of the civilization possessed by all the European populations; it was drawn from the common fountain of Atlantis. (pp. 133-35)

From his discourse on the origin or transmission of civilization, Donnelly goes on to insist that because civilization cannot spring into existence, one cannot argue for an accidental development of parallel civilizations in two worlds, but must look for the common origin from whence both came. Thus, the existence and use of fermented spirits, the use of such architectural devices as the arch, the prevalence of such customs as marriage, of belief in ghosts and deities, the existence of games as similar as the *pachisi* of the Hindu and the *patoli* of the Aztec all indicate to Donnelly the absurdity of believing that "there was no relationship between them, and that they had never had any ante-Columbian intercourse with each other" (p. 163).

Donnelly continues to marshal the evidence: the record of pre-Columbian legends and art; similarities in color and complexion between the peoples of Old World and New; parallels in language and writing, including phonetic alphabets and parallels in the formations of letters and hieroglyphics. Finally, in two of the most difficult and tenuous explications, he insists that not only does Genesis, in its emphasis upon the Chosen People, monotheism, and divine justice, contain corroboration of a continuity from antiquity to the present, but the continuity of Judaism and the Jewish people and their "offspring, Christianity, is taking possession of the habitable world; and the continuous life of one people—one poor, obscure, and wretched people—spans the tremendous gap between 'Ptah-hotep' and this nineteenth century" (p. 213).

In Part IV Donnelly pursues parallels between the mythologies and traditions of the past as they record memories of Atlantis: the Adites of the Arabs, prehistoric men of giant stature, whose parallels are found in the legends of the Hebrews, Persians, Hindus, Egyptians, Mexicans, and others; practices such as the ritual deformation of the skull in primitive peoples; the parallels between Olympus and Atlantis and among the cosmogonies of the Phoenicians, Jews, and Christians; parallel emphases upon articles of commodity, utility, and value from the earliest times to the present; the evolution of a commerce and a colonial system that extended to the ends of the earth, thus making inevitable the dissemination of ideas, values, and beliefs, and the perpetuation of a memory of the origins of all things.

As Donnelly describes them, most of these gifts were obviously beneficial; however, no agrarian, no populist, no sworn enemy of the vested interests of post–Civil War America could fail to recognize that the Atlanteans transmitted a reverence for that which was destined to corrupt as well as to elevate men:

And thus it has come to pass that, precisely as the physicians of Europe, fifty years ago, practiced bleeding, because for thousands of years their savage ancestors had used it to draw away the evil spirits out of the man, so the business of our modern civilization is dependent upon the superstition of a past civilization, and the bankers of the world are to-day perpetuating the adoration of "the tears wept by the sun" which was commenced ages since on the island of Atlantis.

And it becomes a grave question—when we remember that the rapidly increasing business of the world, consequent upon an increasing population, and a civilization advancing with giant steps, is measured by the standard of a currency limited by natural laws, decreasing annually in production, and incapable of expanding proportionately to the growth of the world—whether this Atlantean superstition may not yet inflict more incalculable injuries on mankind than those which resulted from the practice of phlebotomy. (p. 347)

Finally, in the last part of the book, Donnelly defines the means by which the civilization of Atlantis had been transmitted to the civilized parts of the ancient world: by a vast system of colonies that, radiating from the central, strategic position at the mouth of the Mediterranean and pointing the way to the Americas, effectively dominated and directed the development of a world immeasurably greater than the known worlds of the Greeks, the Romans, and others. The Atlanteans, he insists, attempted to conquer it all. He concludes, then, first with a look back across the centuries: "It is not surprising that when this mighty nation sank beneath the waves, in the midst of terrible convulsions, with all its millions of people, the event left an everlasting impression upon the imagination of mankind" (p. 478). Then he looks to the future:

We are but beginning to understand the past: one hundred years ago the world knew nothing of Pompeii or Herculaneum; nothing of the lingual tie that binds together the Indo-European nations; nothing of the significance of the vast volume of inscriptions upon the tombs and temples of Egypt; nothing of the meaning of the arrow-headed inscriptions of Babylon; nothing of the marvelous civilizations revealed in the remains of Yucatan, Mexico, and Peru. We are on the threshold. Scientific investigation is advancing with giant strides. Who shall say that one hundred years from now the great museums of the world may not be adorned with gems, statues, arms, and implements from Atlantis, while the libraries of the world shall contain translations of its inscriptions, throwing new light upon all the past history of the human race, and all the great problems which now perplex the thinkers of our day! (p. 480)

The remarkableness of this intellectual and literary *tour de force* is as evident today as it was in Donnelly's own. Its immediate result was an unexpected but immensely gratifying popular success that eventually resulted in the publication, by 1890, of twenty-three American and twenty-six English editions, and it has remained popular, as continued republications make evident. The reasons for this immediate popularity as well as for the interest that continues are readily apparent: here, in an authoritative, documented, illustrated, and logical synthesis is a comprehensive, imaginative, and exciting explanation for a wide range of curiosities, phenomena, and speculations that had accumulated alternately to perplex and to stimulate the curiosity of the generations who had had the opportunity to assess the tremendous amount of data, most of it uncorrelated, since the rise of the new science. In fewer than five hundred pages, each item is put into its place, its relationships made clear, in a fashion science had led the man of the nineteenth century to expect. The sheer mass of detail included is almost overwhelming, the scholarship is at least initially impressive, and the story told is, if true, the single great story of human history. The theme is a great one, worthy of an age that had tamed time, distance, and darkness for the first time.

Simultaneously, the work is incredibly imaginative, so much so that it is often as dramatic and compelling as a work of fiction, a great romantic tale that, like the works of Donnelly's contemporary, Jules Verne, moves from a basis in possibility to the farthest limits of human probability. It is no coincidence that in Verne's *Twenty Thousand Leagues Under the Sea*, published twelve years earlier, Captain Nemo visits the ruins of Atlantis in his remarkable submarine, the *Nautilus*.

Most impressive, then and now, are the book's style and structure. The evidence, however impressive, is uneven, but it is presented with force and vigor; the tone is that of the debater rather than the scientist, and the evidence is presented much as a lawyer or a politician makes his case before a jury or the electorate. The atmosphere of the book is dominated by an apparent candor that lets no evidence, however minute or contradictory, escape the wide-ranging intellect of the author.

Nevertheless, the shortcomings of the book are more evident now than at the time of its publication—although the scientific community of the time would not condescend to acknowledge its presence, much less its significance. Its apparent relationship to the relentless amassing of evidence that had produced *On the Origin of Species* (1859) is evident, but more evident is its relationship to what David Starr Jordon has characterized as the "systematized ignorance" of pseudoscience, particularly in its uncritical acceptance of testimony it finds useful and its equally uncritical rejection of that which it does not. Particularly weak, in the context of Donnelly's time and our own, is the implicit rejection of Darwinism and all that it has taught us about the nature of change. Donnelly insists that reality, until recently, has been marked by corruption of the original rather than its constant natural refinement, as defined by Darwin and his followers, and that such corruption was sparked by sudden, revolutionary cataclysm rather than gradual, if uneven, evolution.

Nevertheless, in spite of the weakness apparent then and now, the book was extremely important for Donnelly at the time. As welcome as was its financial success, even more pleasing was its personal impact. Even Donnelly's old enemies on the *St. Paul Pioneer Press* were moved to comment without tongue in cheek in the issue of February 18, 1882, that the book showed "an instance of what marvelous force may be imparted to any theory by the simple application of intellectual power." More remarkable was Donnelly's receipt of a four-page complimentary letter postmarked London and signed W. E. Gladstone. The letter prompted him to speculate on "the appearance of the man who, in this little snowbound hamlet, was corresponding with the man whose word was fate anywhere in the British Empire. . . . The leg of my pants was torn; my coat was nearly buttonless. . . . I could have uttered a war whoop of exultation."[2]

Perhaps as a result of his pleasure with the effect he had created in *Atlantis*, Donnelly was already, in the spring of 1882, at work on his next book. This work, which he finished in a scant two months, was called *Ragnarok: The Age of Fire and Gravel*. Working at high speed, he finished the manuscript in seven weeks, and he recorded in his diary that "It grew within me from small beginnings like an inspiration, and I hope it may do some good in the world."[3]

II   Ragnarok: The Age of Fire and Gravel

The relationship between *Ragnarok* and *Atlantis* as well as that between it and most of Donnelly's later works, particularly his fiction, is immediately evident. *Ragnarok* has as its central thesis Donnelly's conviction that change is largely cataclysmic rather than evolutionary in nature, and that, consequently, not only can social change be best explained or predicted in terms of social calamity—as he was to demonstrate in *Doctor Huguet* and *Caesar's Column*—but radical natural change is the result of natural calamity. Thus, just as Donnelly insisted in the earlier work that Atlantis disappeared through a natural disaster, in this one he looks for natural disaster as the explanation of the origin of "The Drift," that mantle of loose rock and till that covers much of the earth's surface. It is obvious that Donnelly assembled the research and conjecture that led to writing *Ragnarok* largely in his attempt to discover the nature of the cataclysm that destroyed Atlantis.

The relationship between the structure of *Ragnarok* and that of *Atlantis* is equally evident. This book too is presented in the manner of a lawyer's brief, focusing first upon the nature of the drift, then upon its possible causes and prerequisites, drawing the conclusion that the most logical cause was the approach of a comet to the earth. Then, through an examination of myth and legend, together with interpreted physical evidence and an extension of his *Atlantis* conclusions, Donnelly insists that logic dictates acceptance of his theory.

In Part I, "The Drift," Donnelly examines the nature of the drift, its extent, and the scientific theories advanced to explain its nature, distribution, and origins. The first he describes in the graphic style that he uses throughout the book:

> Upon the top of the last of this series of stratified rocks we find The Drift. What is it?
>
> Go out with me where yonder men are digging a well. Let us observe the material they are casting out.
>
> First they penetrate through a few inches or a foot or two of surface soil; then they enter a vast deposit of sand, gravel, and clay. It may be fifty, one hundred, five hundred, eight hundred feet, before they reach the stratified rocks on which this drift rests. It covers whole continents. It is our earth. It makes the basis of our soils; our railroads cut their way through it; our carriages drive over it; our cities are built upon it; our crops are derived from it; the water we drink percolates through it; on it we live, love, marry, raise children, think, dream and die; and in the bosom of it we will be buried.[4]

After this attention-capturing, sensational, and relevant opening, Donnelly modestly poses the question, "Where did it come from?" and then suggests, again in tones reminiscent of the trial lawyer,

That is what I propose to discuss with you in this work—if you will have the patience to follow me.

So far as possible [as I shall in all cases speak by the voices of others,] I shall summon my witnesses that you may cross examine them. I shall try, to the best of my ability, to buttress every opinion with adequate proofs. If I do not convince, I hope at least to interest you. (p. 2)

The modesty of Donnelly's disclaimer is particularly evident in comparison both to his description of the extent of the drift and the scope of the evidence that he plans to marshal: "If the theories advanced are gigantic, the facts they seek to explain are not less so. We are not dealing with little things: the phenomena are continental, world-wide, globe-embracing" (p. 7). The theories advanced, the origin of the drift in the action of flood waters, of icebergs, of glaciers, and of a continental ice sheet, are, Donnelly points out, all massive theories, each of which has its vocal supporters and deniers, and each of which is worthy of examination in turn.

The theory that the drift results from wave action is, Donnelly points out, "almost universally abandoned"; that it is the result of icebergs is "simply impossible"; that it results from glaciers is unlikely because of the limited locations of glaciers in relation to the location of the drift; that it originated in continental ice sheets, the most commonly accepted explanation, is as unlikely as a glacial origin for the same reasons multiplied several times.

In each case Donnelly offers substantial evidence to support his conclusion, and the more likely theory—that of continental ice-sheet origin—is refuted by considerably more evidence than the other three. Each bit of evidence is carefully selected for a particular place in a particular argument rather than for its contribution to the theory that he plans to introduce. Thus, his refutation of the wave-origin theory is supported by the evidence of those who accept the continental ice-sheet theory, as are his refutations of the iceberg and the glacier origin theories. His refutation of the continental ice-sheet theory is based on careful selection from those same authorities, reinforced by observations on the extent of the drift. His summary is succinct and clear:

In brief, the Drift is *not* found where ice must have been, and *is* found where ice could not have been; the conclusion, therefore, is irresistible that the Drift is not due to ice. (p. 42)

From this point Donnelly turns to proving what is rather than what is not, and his careful selection of documentary evidence continues to be as controlled as it had been. First, he insists that the Drift fell upon a fair and lovely world, a world far better adapted to give happiness to its inhabitants than this storm-tossed planet on which we now live, with its endless battle between heat and cold, between sun and ice. (p. 43)

This golden age, curiously like that of Atlantis, was disrupted and destroyed as suddenly as Donnelly insisted that island empire had been, and the Drift suddenly covered the land so completely that forests of living trees were covered and preserved for discovery in our own day. Further, Donnelly insists that all evidence suggests that the catastrophe was characterized not by great cold, as the proponents of the continental ice-sheet theory insist, but by great heat, the dissipation of which may then, in turn, have precipitated the ice age that followed.

At this point, Donnelly directs his arguments carefully, insuring that each makes its contribution to only one possible conclusion:

What, now, are the elements of the problem to be solved?
First, we are to find something that instantaneously increased to a vast extent the heat of our planet, vaporized the seas, and furnished the material for deluges of rain, and great storms of snow, and accumulations of ice north and south of the equator and in the high mountains.
Secondly, we are to find something that, coming from above, smashed, pounded, and crushed "as with a maul," and rooted up as with a plow, the gigantic rocks of the surface, and scattered them for hundreds of miles from their original location.
Thirdly, we are to find something which brought to the planet vast, incalculable masses of clay and gravel, which did not contain any of the earth's fossils; . . . which are marked after a fashion which cannot be found anywhere else on earth. . . .
Fourthly, we are to find something that would produce cyclonic convulsions upon a scale for which the ordinary operations of nature furnish us no parallel.
Fifthly, we are to find some external force so mighty that it would crack the crust of the globe like an eggshell, lining its surface with great rents and seams, through which the molten interior boiled up to the light. (pp. 63–64)

Having summarized and recapitulated the conclusions drawn from his evidence, Donnelly needs now only to draw the ultimate conclusion and to demonstrate its validity:

Would a comet meet all these prerequisites?
I think it would.
Let us proceed in regular order.

Donnelly then proceeds, in his "regular order," to support his conjecture, all of the evidence included playing its appointed part in fleshing out his thesis, making agreement virtually inevitable. His proof is divided into three parts, each represented by a section of the book: "The Comet," which deals with the nature of the comet and its presumed effect in an earthly collision or near miss; "The Legends," which explores mythological and biblical parallels that lend themselves to his interpretation; and "Conclusions," which not only sums up his arguments but includes his theories on the relationships between the effect of the comet and man's survival.

The result is, like *Atlantis*, a remarkable compendium of bits and pieces of information fashioned into a meaningful whole. And the meaningful whole that Donnelly constructs is his initial conviction that the drift is the result of a collision or near miss between the earth and a comet. Perhaps the single most significant factor in his presentation, certainly more effective than the evidence itself, is the care with which Donnelly selected that evidence.

Donnelly's citations of scientific data concerning the physical nature of comets are reasonably accurate insofar as the state of the science was precise at the time Donnelly wrote, but again his selection from that data was crucial, as his summary of that evidence makes clear:

I.   Comets consist of a blazing nucleus and a mass of ponderable, separated matter, such as stones, gravel, clay-dust, and gas.
II. The nucleus gives out great heat and masses of burning gas.
III. Luminous gases surround the nucleus. (p. 80)

To this summary are added his earlier conclusions:

IV. The drift-clays are the result of the grinding up of granitic rocks.
V.   No such deposits, of anything like equal magnitude, could have been formed on the earth.
VI. No such clays are now being formed under glaciers or Arctic ice-sheets. (pp. 80–81)
VII. These clays were ground out of the substance of the comet by the endless changes of position of the material of which it is composed as it flew through space, during its incalculable journeys in the long reaches of time. (p. 81)

Other earlier conclusions suggest a similar explanation:

VIII. The earth-supplies of gravel are inadequate to account for the gravel of the drift deposits.

IX. Neither sea-beach nor rivers produce stones like those found in the Drift. (p. 81)

Donnelly moves further into conjecture as he examines the likelihood of a comet striking the earth and the consequences if that collision had taken place. As he does so, Donnelly becomes increasingly imaginative in his description, seeking to convince the reader of the feasibility of his idea:

Look out at the scene around you. Here are trees fifty feet high. Imagine an instantaneous descent of granite-sand and gravel sufficient to smash and crush those trees to the ground, to bury their trunks, and to cover the earth one hundred to five hundred feet higher than the elevation to which their tops now reach! And this not alone here in your garden, or over your farm, or over your township, or over your county, or over your state; but over the whole continent in which you dwell—in short, over the greater part of the habitable world. . . .

But, lo! through the darkness, the wretches not beaten down and overwhelmed in the debris, but scurrying to mountain-caves for refuge, have a new terror: the cry passes from lip to lip, "The world is on fire!" (pp. 107–108)

The human reactions to this catastrophe are not merely imaginative descriptions, however; in the bulk of the book, providing almost all of what Donnelly considers to be direct evidence, is a thorough discussion of the nature of myth and the mythical evidence for accepting his theory. In discussions that seem to be remarkably contemporary, particularly to those literary critics who examine myth patterns and repetitions, Donnelly discussed the nature and reliability of myth. First he discusses origins:

. . . In primitive races mind repeats mind for thousands of years. If a tale is told at a million hearth-fires, the probabilities are small, indeed, that any innovation at one hearth-fire, however ingenious, will work its way into and modify at all the rest. There is no printing-press to make the thoughts of one man the thoughts of thousands. While the innovator is modifying the tale, to his own satisfaction, to his immediate circle of hearers, the narrative is being repeated in its unchanged form at all the rest. The doctrine of chances is against innovation. The majority rules.

When, however, a marvelous tale is told to the new generation . . . they naturally ask, "Where did all this occur?" The narrator must satisfy this curiosity, and so he replies, "On yonder mountain top," or "In yonder cave."

The story has come down without its geography, and a new geography is given it. . . .

But, as a rule, simple races repeat; they do not invent. (pp. 114–15)

Equally interesting and deliberately prophetic is Donnelly's prediction of the increased use of mythical evidence in the future, a
prediction pragmatically designed to support his argument, yet quite
accurate in foreseeing the rise of myth scholarship:

In the future, more and more attention will be given to the myths of
primitive races; they will be accounted as more reliable, and as reaching
farther back in time than many things which we call history. Thoughtful men
will analyze them, despising nothing; like a chemist who resolves some
compound object into its original elements—the very combination constituting a history of the object. (pp. 117–18)

All this discussion of the nature and future role of myth is,
however, pointed: it is prefatory to Donnelly's use of mythical
materials to produce direct evidence from eye witnesses to that great
catastrophe, evidence that has been preserved for us, sometimes in
direct, literal form, but more frequently in metaphors.

Before assessing that mythical evidence, however, Donnelly digresses to establish an important fact: that man did exist on the earth
before the coming of the drift, and hence having witnessed it, was
capable of preserving its memory from generation to generation and
from place to place. Using archaeological evidence to support his
insistence that man did antedate the drift on the earth, he summar-
izes:

Remember that the Drift is unfossiliferous and un-stratified; that it fell *en
masse*, and that these remains are found in its lower part, or caught between it
and the rocks below it, and you can form a vivid picture of the sudden and
terrible catastrophe. The trees were imbedded with man and the animals; the
bones of men, smaller and more friable, probably perished, ground up in the
tempest, while only their flint implements and the great bones of the larger
animals, hard as stones, remain to tell the dreadful story. And yet some
human bones have been found. . . . (pp. 123–24)

After having "given enough [evidence] to satisfy the reader that
man *did* exist before the Drift," Donnelly turns to the legends
themselves, attempting to divide them chronologically so that the
various stages—the coming of the comet, the impact, and the
aftermath—may be made clear through this human testimony. First
he presents legends that tell, metaphorically or literally, of "the first
coming of the monster, the dragon, the serpent, the wolf, the dog, the
Evil One, the Comet," as it appears in various forms. His quotation
from *Mythology of the British Druids* is typical of this use, as is his
explanation. First, Donnelly quotes:

"The profligacy of mankind had provoked the great Supreme to send a pestilential *wind* upon the earth. *A pure poison descended, every blast was death.* At this time the patriarch, distinguished for his integrity, *was shut up,* together with his select company, in the *inclosure with the strong door.* (The cave?) Here the just ones were safe from injury. *Presently a tempest of fire arose. It split the earth asunder* to the great deep. The lake Llion burst its bounds, and the waves of the sea lifted themselves on high around the borders of Britain, *the rain poured down from heaven, and the waters covered the earth.*" (p. 135; italics Donnelly's)

Donnelly follows this citation with what he sees as the logical interpretation:

Here we have the whole story told briefly, but with the regular sequence of events:
1. The poisonous gases.
2. The people seek shelter in the caves.
3. The earth takes fire.
4. The earth is cleft open; the fiords are made, and the trap-rocks burst forth.
5. The rain pours down.
6. There is a season of floods. (p. 135)

Central to Donnelly's argument is that special myth which gives its title to his book: the Scandinavian myth called "Ragnarok," long considered to be "the darkness of the gods." Donnelly discusses in detail the implications for his thesis:

The very name is significant. According to Professor Anderson's etymology of the word, it means "the darkness of the gods"; from *regin*, gods, and *rokr*, darkness; but it may, more properly, be derived from the Icelandic, Danish, and Swedish *regn*, a rain, and *rok*, smoke or dust; and it may mean the *rain of dust*, for the clay came first as dust; it is described in some Indian legends as ashes. (p. 141)

The reinterpretation of the etymology of Ragnarok sets the pattern for Donnelly's reinterpretation of the myth itself, as he selects those portions that lend themselves to such interpretation and at the same time tell the story of the catastrophe. For Donnelly, the retelling is essentially a matter of translating metaphor into realistic description, much as he had done in earlier discussions in this book and in *Atlantis.* The source of the catastrophe, like that which destroyed Atlantis, has its origins in crime and punishment, a moral dimension that has its parallels in other mythical tales of destruction and regeneration:

First, there is, as in the tradition of the Druids . . . the story of an age of crime.

The Vala looks upon the world, and, as the "Elder Edds" tells us—

"There saw she wade
In the heavy streams,
Men—foul murderers
And perjurers,
And them who others' wives
Seduce to sin.
Brothers slay brothers;
Sisters' children
Shed each other's blood.
Hard is the world!
Sensual sin grows huge.
There are sword-ages, axe-ages;
Shields are cleft in twain;
Storm-ages, murder ages;
Till the world falls dead,
And men no longer spare
Or pity one another."

(Anderson, "Norse Mythology," p. 416).

The world has ripened for destruction; and "Ragnarok," the darkness of the gods, or the rain of dust and ashes, comes to complete the work. . . .

"There are three winters," or years, "during which great wars rage over the world." Mankind has reached a climate of wickedness. . . .

"Then happens that which will seem a great miracle: that *the wolf devours the sun*, and this will seem a great loss."

That is, the Comet strikes the sun, or approaches so close to it that it seems to do so.

"The other wolf devours the moon, and this, too, will cause great mischief."

We have seen that the comets often come in couples or triplets.

"The stars shall be hurled from heaven."

This refers to the blazing *debris* of the Comet falling to the earth.

"Then it shall come to pass that the earth will shake so violently that trees will be torn up by the roots, the mountains will topple down, and all the bonds and fetters will be broken and snapped."

Chaos has come again. How closely does all this agree with Hesiod's description of the shaking earth and the universal conflict of nature?

"The Fenris-wolf gets loose."

This, we shall see, is the name of one of the comets.

"*The sea rushes over the earth*, for the Midgard-serpent writhes in giant rage, and seeks to gain the land."

The Midgard-serpent is the name of another comet; it strives to reach the earth; its proximity disturbs the oceans. . . . (pp. 141–43; italics Donnelly's)

Donnelly continues to trace the movement of the comets and their impact on earth through the metaphors of the myths. The gods are awakened and come to the defense of men, but one of them is "poisoned by the venom that the serpent blows upon him," or, in Donnelly's view, "He has breathed the carburated-hydrogen gas!" (p. 143). Ultimately, however, the serpents retreat, men reappear on the earth, and

> "The fields unsown
> Yield their growth;
> All ills cease.
> Balder comes.
> Hader and Balder,
> Those heavenly gods,
> Dwell together in Odin's halls."

(p. 153)

Or, in Donnelly's interpretation,

> The great catastrophe is past. Man is saved. The world is once more fair. The sun shines again in heaven. Night and day follow each other in endless revolution around the happy globe. Ragnarok is past. (p. 153)

Donnelly turns then to other legends: those of the Romans, the Central American Toltecs, the Aztecs, the ancient Persians, the Hindus, and of ten or more Indian tribes. He concludes that "we must concede that these legends of a world-embracing conflagration represent a race-remembrance of a great fact, or that they are a colossal falsehood—an invention of man" (p. 193).

He goes on to trace other legends from a variety of sources, those that deal with an Age of Darkness, of the Triumph of the Sun, and of the Fall of Clay and Gravel. In Deuteronomy (chapter 28) he finds further support:

> "22. The Lord shall smite thee . . . with an extreme burning, and with the sword, and with blasting, and with mildew; and they shall pursue thee until thou perish.
> "23. And thy heaven that is over thy head shall be brass, and the earth that is under thee shall be iron.
> "24. *The Lord shall make the rain of the land powder and dust: from heaven shall it come down upon thee, until thou be destroyed.* . . .
> "29. And thou shalt *grope at noonday*, as the blind gropeth in darkness." (p. 263; italics Donnelly's)

In the most remarkable chapters in the book, Donnelly reads the books of Job and Genesis in terms of his theory of the comet, concluding his interpretation of Job with the assertion that the God who tried Job was he who sent

the crooked serpents with which God had adorned the heavens: . . . the monster with blazing head casting out jets of light, breathing volumes of smoke, molten, shining, brilliant, irresistible, against whom man hurled their weapons in vain; for destruction went before him; he cast down stones and pointed things upon the mire, the clay. . . . This is he whose rain of fire killed Job's sheep and shepherds; whose chaotic winds killed Job's children. . . . (p. 313)

Genesis, Donnelly points out, is an even more elaborate metaphor, in which is recorded

1. The Golden Age; the Paradise.
2. The universal moral degeneracy of mankind; the age of crime and violence.
3. God's vengeance.
4. The serpent; the fire from heaven.
5. The cave—life and the darkness.
6. The cold; the struggle to live.
7. The "Fall of Man," from virtue to vice; from plenty to poverty; from civilization to barbarism; from the Tertiary to the Drift; from Eden to the gravel.
8. Reconstruction and regeneration.
   Can all this be accidental? Can all this mean nothing? (p. 340)

The last part of the book, "Conclusions," is largely anticlimax, as Donnelly restates his conviction that preglacial man had reached a high degree of civilization, much of which was destroyed by the catastrophe; that a preglacial continent, obviously Atlantis, had been destroyed at the same time; that all the evidence he has amassed in his attempt to validate his theory is also testimony to man's durability, to his ability to rise above adversity and catastrophe.

Donnelly ends *Ragnarok* with a plea for man to seek understanding and to open his mind to the great possibilities for intellectual progress. He concludes didactically, as though he were ending a long homily or a plea before a jury:

. . . Widen your heart. Put your intellect to work to so readjust the values of labor and increase the productive capacity of Nature, that plenty and happiness, light and hope, may dwell in every heart, and the Catacombs be closed for ever.

And from such a world God will fend off the comets with his great right arm, and the angels will exult over it in heaven. (p. 441)

The diversity, the attempted profundity, and the dubious science, all of which abound in *Ragnarok,* combine to make it easy to ridicule Donnelly, particularly from the perspective of a century later; and the literal acceptance of this book as well as *Atlantis* by a variety of cultists tempts one to dismiss both as ridiculous. But such a dismissal would be unfair to both the book and its author, and it would mislead a good many potential readers who might otherwise find the qualities that give the book a measure of relevance even yet.

Less important than the scientific inaccuracies (and Donnelly's science is highly debatable when it is not impossible, improbable, or downright wrong) is the vividness of Donnelly's imagination, a vividness that provides the nonbelieving reader with a work that can, like the Old Testament, be read as a gigantic metaphor of man's rise, fall, and regeneration—actually in the same way that Donnelly himself reads scripture. The result, in this sense, is a rewarding trip through Donnelly's imagination into man's remote past, just as his imagination was to take the readers of his later novels into man's future.

This is not to say, however, that whatever faults the work displays can be overlooked, particularly as they recur in Donnelly's future writing. Perhaps the most serious of these faults, particularly in view of his determination to organize the work and its presentation of evidence as carefully as a legal brief, is the habit of pursuing digressions, particularly those that contribute less of substance than their detraction from the flow of the work justifies. As in his other works, earlier and later, Donnelly wrote rapidly and did little rewriting, and this book, like most of the others, would have benefited by a careful, extensive pruning.

Nevertheless, the book is important to any attempt to understand Donnelly's thinking, displaying as it does his conviction that all of nature grows in cycles, that those cycles are punctuated or accelerated by gigantic catastrophes, and that consequently there are natural limits inherent in man's ability to progress. This conviction was not only dangerous for one who was ostensibly a complete, dedicated reformer, but in the final analysis it placed a permanent limit on his faith in man, in man's ability to progress, and in the vision of the future that, since the eighteenth century, reformers and idealists had relished for giving man a confidence in his control over his life, his government, and his destiny.

Interestingly, Donnelly linked his concept of Ragnarok—the

twilight of the gods or the rain of dust and gravel, a natural catastrophe—to traditional religious concepts that he had ignored for years but that had, perhaps unconsciously, affected much of his thinking. One of these was the age-old belief that everything happens according to God's plan and for the best:

Although it seems that many times have comets smitten the earth, covering it with *debris*, or causing its rocks to boil, and its waters to ascend into the heavens, yet, considering all life, as revealed in the fossils, from the first cell unto this day, *nothing has perished* that *was worth preserving.*
So far as we can judge, after every cataclysm the world has risen to higher levels of creative development. (p. 438)

The second traditional concept is even more interesting for its persistence in Donnelly's thinking:

If we fall again upon
                    "Axe-ages, sword-ages,
                    Wind ages, murder-ages"—
if "sensual sins grow huge"; if "brother spoils brother"; if Sodom and Gomorrah come again—who can say that God may not bring out of the depths of space a rejuvenating comet? (p. 439)

Three days after finishing *Ragnarok* Donnelly began another book, "God and the Sun." But he did not complete it, perhaps initially because of exhaustion, but then more certainly because of reaction to *Ragnarok.*
If the reception of *Atlantis* pleased Donnelly, that of *Ragnarok* had the opposite effect. Not only had it been rejected by Harper and Brothers, who had published *Atlantis*, and by Scribner's, but it was met when at last published (by Appleton) first by adverse criticism and then by silence. Its theories were roundly rejected by the scientific community, the editor of *Popular Science* calling it "absurd," and the *Chicago Tribune* could only comment favorably on Donnelly's industriousness but not upon his scholarship. Convinced that a nonprofessional could not receive a fair hearing from the scientific community, Donnelly turned again to politics and to speculation.

CHAPTER 4

Secrets of the Past and Future

D ONNELLY'S excursion into scientific polemics had been the
result of his fears that his political life had run its course. But in
the summer of 1882 he turned down an invitation to seek the nomination for Congress as a liberal Democrat, and in the fall of that
year he campaigned actively for the party's nominee, enjoying his role
as crowd-pleaser tremendously.

Although he insisted that he had left politics for literature, he
remained absorbed in political affairs, speaking to the newly formed
Minnesota Farmers' Alliance at their convention in 1885. Earlier, in
1884, a movement began within that group to draft him as a
congressional candidate. By the middle of the summer Donnelly was
in the midst of putting together a coalition of Democrat, People's
party, Liberal Republican, and Farmers' Alliance forces to nominate
a candidate for the House. On August 19, the alliance nominated
him, and the campaign seemed assured of success. But even as Grover
Cleveland was winning the presidency, Minnesota remained Republican. Donnelly lost by fewer than 1,000 votes out of 32,000 cast, but
his efforts to secure patronage support from the Cleveland adminis-
tration for himself and others came to nothing.

So involved had Donnelly again become in politics that he now
wrote to a friend that he could not live without office. But he
nonetheless continued the literary career he had begun with *Atlantis*,
and through much of 1884 he was absorbed by a new project, which
he pursued with the determination that had marked his earlier
ventures, convinced that the same techniques he had employed in the
earlier works would prove successful in the newer. His confidence
was based on his conviction that he had the evidence to demolish one
of the most sacred of literary sacred cows.

I The Great Cryptogram

As early as 1873, Donnelly had begun to speculate on the true
authorship of Shakespeare's plays, because he believed that neither

the scanty information about Shakespeare nor the evidence of his even scantier education supported continued belief in his having created such masterful art. By 1878 he became convinced that somewhere in the plays might be discovered a cryptogram that would reveal their true author, a brilliant but anonymous Elizabethan.

Finally he decided that Francis Bacon, who was interested in ciphers, was the true author of the plays. While working on *Atlantis* and *Ragnarok* Donnelly continued his speculation: in the former book he referred to Bacon as "a profoundly wise and great man," and in the latter he made clear his skepticism about Shakespeare's authorship. On September 23, 1882, he recorded in his diary that he had discovered the key to the cipher.

While continuing his active role in politics—especially during his unsuccessful campaign for Congress in 1884—he began work on what was to be called *The Great Cryptogram: Francis Bacon's Cipher in the So-Called Shakespeare Plays.* It was published by R. S. Peale of Chicago in the fall of 1887, just as Donnelly was finally elected to the state legislature as a Farmers' Alliance candidate. The book received a good deal of advance publicity, its publication was conducted in strict security, and it gave Donnelly a good deal of notoriety on both sides of the Atlantic. Its initial effect was to please Baconians and to contribute to Donnelly's growing reputation for eccentricity; but it also led Donnelly to his first reception abroad as a scholar, as well as an eccentric, and an invitation to debate at Oxford.

The book is Donnelly's most detailed as well as his most carefully organized, from the superscript on the title page, that passage from *Henry IV, Part I*, Act I, Scene 3, with its cryptic reference to the "unsteadfast footing of a Spear," to his final defense of Bacon's character against the many attacks made upon it both by his contemporaries and by historians of the two and a half centuries that followed.

Donnelly begins and ends the book with an apology, initially that the book's admitted imperfections are the result of the many distractions imposed by an active career, and finally that he had been persuaded to rush it into print before it had been made perfect because of his initial public announcement in 1884 that he had found the cipher. But nowhere does he apologize for his principal assertion—the focal point of the book—that a cipher exists, that it provides a continuous narrative through the plays, and that he has discovered the numerical key by which it can be deciphered.

The volume is divided into three books: I, The Argument; II, The Demonstration; and III, Conclusions. The first two books are divided into two or more parts, and each part contains from five to twenty-two chapters. This complex organization, as tedious as it is meticulous, is the culmination of the technique for marshaling and presenting evidence that Donnelly had developed in *Atlantis* and continued in *Ragnarok*: the book is essentially a legal brief constructed to prove conclusively, first, that Shakespeare could not have written the plays; second, that Bacon could have done so; and third, that the cipher gives conclusive evidence that Bacon had written them.

Throughout the work Donnelly makes a clear and careful distinction between William *Shakspere*, the man from Stratford, who spelled his name that way in his will, and William *Shakespeare*, the name on the title pages of the quartos and folios as they appeared. Donnelly's intent is obvious: from the beginning he is determined to emphasize the existence of two persons, the rustic from Stratford and the urban author.

The title of Book I, Part I, makes clear, then, Donnelly's initial position: "William Shakspere Did Not Write the Plays," an assertion based almost entirely upon the apparent lack of learning evident in what is known of Shakspere of Stratford and the obviously great learning evident in the plays. Donnelly begins by citing summary statements from many of the traditional authorities: Voltaire, who called Shakespeare a "drunken savage"; Pope, "a man of no education"; Richard Grant White, "this bewitching but untutored and half-savage child of nature"; Milton, that he "warbled his native wood-notes wild"; Ben Jonson, that he possessed "small Latin and less Greek"; Thomas Fuller, who said that "his learning was very little."[1]

Contrary to these traditional assertions, however, Donnelly points out the general conclusion of scholars in his own century concerning the nature of the author:

> But in the last fifty years this view is completely changed. The critical world is now substantially agreed that the man who wrote the plays was one of the most learned men of the world, not only in that learning which comes from observation and reflection, but in book-lore, ancient and modern, and in the knowledge of many languages. (p. 14)

This later conclusion is critical to Donnelly's entire argument, because unless he can substantiate the existence of two men, the unlettered rustic who could not have written the plays, and the learned scholar who did, there is no need for proving either the existence or secret of a cipher in the plays. This he proceeds to do, first by documenting the learning evident in the plays and then examining the limited education available to Shakespeare. Much, but certainly not all, of his evidence is circumstantial, dealing with the nature of the times in the small towns, a situation from which he is able to make obvious, acceptable deductions. He points out, for example that—

> The people of Stratford were densely ignorant. At the time of Shakspere's birth only six aldermen of the town, out of nineteen, could write their names; and of the thirteen who could not write, Shakspere's father, John Shakspere, was one. . . .
>
> Shakspere's whole family were illiterate. He was the first of his race that we know of who was able to read and write. His father and mother, grandfathers and grandmothers, aunts and cousins—all signed their names, on the few occasions when they were obliged to sign them, with crosses. His daughter Judith could not read or write. The whole population around him were in the same conditions. (p. 29)

Donnelly sums up the effect of such an environment with the pungency he might use as a prosecutor describing that of a prisoner in the dock:

> It would indeed be a miracle if out of this vulgar, dirty, illiterate family came the greatest genius, the profoundest thinker, the broadest scholar that has adorned the annals of the human race. It is possible. It is scarcely probable. (p. 31)

Circumstantial environmental evidence gives way to the little direct evidence and much speculation concerning Shakespeare's education, his opportunity for self-education, and his career in London, where, Donnelly surmises, one might find traces of his learning or his attempts to acquire it. But, Donnelly insists, none is available, either directly or in the traditions or reminiscences of his peers.

Donnelly goes on to examine Shakespeare's character as tradition and evidence, direct and circumstantial, suggest that it was, and he points out the lack of the kinds of material that we might reasonably expect to have survived: letters, books, early or original copies of the plays; he cites the differences, including omissions of parts of the text, between the quartos and the First Folio; he shows contradictions between statements by Ben Jonson and by John Heminge and Henry Condell; he cites the lack of anything connected with the plays in Shakespeare's estate or his will. The evidence that he presents is almost all indirect, but, piled piece on piece, it presents a serious indictment of the traditional belief and a picture of Shakespeare as an unsophisticated, unlettered actor of limited ability and means rather than the traditional image of Shakespeare as the Bard of Stratford, an image so used and overused that it has become a cliché. With his conclusion that the true author of the plays must have had substantial legal training, an impossibility for Shakespeare of Stratford, he turns in Part II to the case for Francis Bacon's authorship.

Whereas Book I, Part I, is essentially a circumstantial indictment and refutation of the traditional assertion that the plays attributed to William Shakespeare were indeed written by William Shakespeare of Stratford, Part II uses essentially the same kind of evidence to demonstrate that Francis Bacon was the true author.

Perhaps most important in Donnelly's argument is his insistence that Bacon's background, training, and experience had prepared him for writing the plays, whereas, as he insisted in Part I, Shakspere's had not. Donnelly's comparisons and contrasts are as vivid as they are conclusive to his lawyer's mind. On the matter of scenes set at sea, for example, he says:

... We are told that this man [Shakespeare], who had never been at sea, wrote the play of *The Tempest*, which contains a very accurate description of the management of a vessel in a storm.
The second Lord Mulgrave gives, in Boswell's edition a communication showing that
Shakespeare's technical knowledge of seamanship must have been the result of the most accurate personal observation, or, what is perhaps more difficult, of the power of combining and applying the information derived from others.
But no books had then been published on the subject. Dr. Johnson says:
His naval dialect is, perhaps, the first example of sailor's language exhibited on the stage.
Lord Mulgrave continues:
The succession of events is strictly observed in the natural progress of the distress described; the expedients adopted are the most proper that could be devised for a chance of safety.... The words of command are strictly proper.... He has shown a knowledge of the new improvements as well as the doubtful points of seamanship.
Capt. Glascock, R. N., says:
The Boatswain, in *The Tempest*, delivers himself in the true vernacular of the forecastle.
All this would, indeed, be most extraordinary in a man who had never been at sea. Bacon, on the other hand, we know to have made two voyages to France; we know how close and accurate were his powers of observation; and in *The Natural History of the Winds* he gives, at great length, a description of the masts and sails of a vessel, with the dimensions of each sail, the mode of handling them, and the necessary measure to be taken in a storm. (p. 172)

Donnelly examines the geography of the plays, concluding that "the place of Bacon's birth and the place of his residence are both made the subjects of scenes in the plays" (p. 172); moreover, he examines the politics displayed in the plays and concludes that

I find the political identities between Bacon and the writer of the Plays to be as follows:
   Both were aristocrats.
   Both despised the mob.
   Both condemned tradesmen.
   Both loved liberty.
   Both loved feudalism. . . . (p. 195)

Finally, after defining thirteen additional similarities, most of them of greater specificity than these, he concludes that "surely, surely, we are getting the two heads under one hat—and that the hat of the great philosopher of Veralam." (p. 195).

Before turning to Book I, Part III, "Parallelisms," Donnelly again sums up the evidence for Bacon:

I have in the foregoing pages shown that, if we treat the real author of the Plays, and Francis Bacon, as two men, they belonged to the same station in society, to the same profession—the law; to the same political party and to the same faction in the state; that they held the same religious views, the same philosophical tenets and the same purposes in life. That each was a poet and a philosopher, a writer of dramatic compositions, and a play-goer. That Bacon had the genius, the opportunity, the time and the necessity to write the Plays, and ample reason to conceal his authorship. (p. 293)

Part III, "Parallelisms," is essentially a study of stylistic similarities between known works by Bacon and the plays, a close examination of expressions, usages, metaphors, phrases, and finally, psychological insights, or, as Donnelly calls them, character insights into the mind of the author of the plays. Again, the evidence, although circumstantial, perhaps even coincidental, is nevertheless, to Donnelly, conclusive evidence of the identity of the author of the plays.

All of Book I, Donnelly's "Argument," is prefatory to Book II, "The Demonstration," although Donnelly admits that to him the evidence is already conclusive that Francis Bacon was indeed the author of the plays. Part I of the second book, "The Cipher in the Plays," is essentially personal narrative, beginning with Donnelly's conviction that, because Bacon wrote the plays, he was proud of them, and because he was familiar with ciphers, he had put one in the plays. Despite that conviction, Donnelly had searched in vain through the plays, finding only suggestions or hints of secrets behind them, until he determined to use as a basis a photostatic copy of the folio of 1623. Even then he endured weeks and months of pondering, reading, and analyzing, until the key to the cipher, the relationship between cipher words and the pages on which they occurred, was revealed to him. From then on his task was based as much on conviction as on faith. In the most engrossing as well as the least ponderous section of the book, Donnelly describes the challenge by comparing it with that of the decipherers of the Rosetta stone:

It seems to me that the labors of Champollion le Jeune and Thomas Young, in working out the Egyptian hieroglyphics from the tri-lingual inscription on the Rosetta stone, were simple compared with the task I had undertaken. They had before them a stone with an inscription in three alphabets. . . . The problem was to translate the unknown by the known. . . .

My problem was to find out, by means of a cipher rule of which I knew little, a cipher story of which I knew less. . . . It was translating into the vernacular an inscription written in an unknown language, with an unknown alphabet, without a single clue, however slight, to the meaning of either. I do not wonder that Bacon said that there are some ciphers which exclude the decipherers. He certainly thought he had constructed one in these Plays. (pp. 575–77)

The cipher story, Donnelly was convinced, would be found in *Henry IV, Part I*, and *Henry IV, Part II*, plays published in 1598 and 1600, respectively, because, he asserts, Bacon first wanted to test possible suspicion in the public at large or among the followers of Robert Cecil, Earl of Salisbury and Elizabeth's secretary of state. To Donnelly the situation was clear:

. . . If it *had* aroused suspicion; if "Francis" "bacon" (printed with a small *b*), "Nicholas" "bacons" (also with a small *b*), "son," "St. Albans," etc., etc., had caught the eye of any of Cecil's superserviceable followers, then he would have held back the second part, and it would have been simply impossible for any person to have worked out the cipher story; because it turned upon pages 73 and 74 of an intended folio, while the quarto copy of the play began with page 1. . . .

And in 1600, after the first part of the play of Henry IV had stood the test of two years of criticism, and the watchful eyes and ears of Francis Bacon could see or hear no sign or sound to indicate that his secret was suspected, he ventured to put forth the second part of the play. But this, like the other began with page 1, and detection was almost impossible. (pp. 577–78)

For Donnelly the key to unlocking the cipher was the Folio of

1623, in which, three years before Bacon's death, the plays were put together as cipher-mates, just as were for the first time the two parts of *Henry IV*. He illustrates his conviction by reproducing from his photographic copy of the Folio of 1623 pages 73 and 74, the end of Part I and the beginning of Part II, from which he deduces the root-numbers of the cipher, those which, he insists, unlock in the two plays the cipher story, a complex retelling of the political and social intrigue of Elizabethan England.

Unfortunately, however, Donnelly's carefully contrived numerical key doesn't quite unlock the cipher, either in the *Henry IV* plays or elsewhere, and Donnelly finds it necessary, even while he constructs parallels between court and political intrigue in the plays and in the England of Bacon's—and Shakespeare's—time, to rely upon assertions and parallels that are, ultimately, circumstantial rather than conclusively factual. Recognizing this inherent weakness, he asserts:

> That the cipher is there; that I have found it out; that the narrative given is real, no man can doubt who reads this book to the end. There may be faults in my workmanship; there are none in the Cipher itself. All that I give is reality; but I may not give all there is. The difficulties are such as arise from the wonderful complexity of the Cipher, and the almost impossibility of the brain holding all the interlocking threads of the root-numbers in their order. Some more mathematical head than mine may be able to do it.
>
> I would call the attention of those who may think that the results are accidental to the fact that each scene, and, in fact, each column and page, tells a different part of the same continuous story. In one place, it is the rage of the Queen; in another, the flight of the actors; in another, Bacon's despair; in another, the village doctor; in another, the description of the sick Shakspere; in another, the supper, etc.—all derived from the same series of numbers used in the same order. (p. 64)

The last chapter of Book II, Part II, is what Donnelly calls "A Word Personal," but it is just one of the many "words personal," essentially statements of faith and conviction with which he ties the book together. Paired with the apology with which he opens the book, this chapter describes the difficulties of the work, particularly after the public announcement that he had found the cipher and the resulting public reaction of skepticism and ridicule. He pleads for the hearing that he insists the theory and the evidence demand. Finally, he appeals to his readers' and critics' sense of mystery and romance:

> Even while the critics are writing their essays, to demonstrate that all I have revealed is a fortuitous combination of coincidence, keen and able minds will

be taking up my imperfect clues and reducing the Cipher to such perfection that it will be as useless to deny the presence of the sun in the heavens as to deny the existence of the inner story in the Plays.

And what a volume of historical truths will roll out of the text. . . . The inner life of kings and queens . . . the struggle of factions in the courts; the interior view of the birth of religions; the first colonization of the American continent . . . the real biography of Essex; the real story of Bacon's career. . . . It will be, in short, the inner story of the most important era in human history, told by the keenest observer and most powerful writer that has ever lived. . . . A great light bursting from a tomb, and covering with its royal effulgence the very cradle of English Literature. (pp. 893–94)

After such a peroration Donnelly might have simply stopped, confident that, as in a law court, he has presented his most eloquent and compelling argument at the end, but he does not. Instead, as at the end of *Atlantis* and *Ragnarok*, he seems unwilling to end at the logical conclusion. Instead, he includes Book III, "Conclusions," which is, in effect, a combined appendix and annotated bibliography in which he discusses the work of other Baconians, including Delia Salter Bacon, whose *Philosophy of the Plays of Shakespeare Unfolded* (1857), with a preface by Nathaniel Hawthorne, first advanced the Baconian theory, supported largely by intuition, and then passed quickly into obscurity. He concludes with "Other Masks of Bacon," in which he "reasons" that Bacon was the author of a dozen other plays of the period, each of which perhaps contributes to the secret history; and finally he refutes those "assaults which have been made upon the good name of Francis Bacon" by his contemporaries and by historians. The Bacon who emerges is, like a prisoner in the dock, defended by an able attorney unafraid of excesses; he is not merely the author of the plays but the great man of Western history whose fate it is to be deprived of his rightful recognition by the spite and envy of the lesser men who surrounded him in his age and followed him since.

The Great Cryptogram is, like the two volumes that preceded it, a legal logician's concept of a case proven. But just as neither *Atlantis* nor *Ragnarok* is good science, neither is *The Great Cryptogram* good cryptography. In *The Codebreakers*, a detailed history of the art and science of cryptography, David Kahn discusses the efforts of Donnelly and other Baconian cipher-hunters in a chapter entitled "The Pathology of Cryptography." Kahn deals essentially with what he calls "cryptanalytic hyperactivity," in which "Its victims over-cryptanalyze documents and they bring forth invalid solutions."[2] Of Donnelly, he writes:

What had he discovered? He found, as he had expected he would, a narrative revealing that *Shak'st spur never writ a word of them* and *It is even thought here that your cousin of St. Albans* [Bacon as Viscount of St. Albans] *writes them.* "Them" referred, of course, to the plays. Some of the decipherment was in the third person; why, Donnelly never explained. How had he discovered all this?

He had begun by misapprehending Bacon's cipher. Based upon this, he had sought an interrelationship of numbers that would locate the words of the hidden message by their serial position on the page or in an act. In its simplest form, the system would, for example, find that the 17th, 18th, 19th, and 20th words on pages 17, 18, 19, and 20 spelled out "I, Bacon, wrote this. . . ."

Of Donnelly's "system" it may be remarked that nothing like it has appeared in cryptology before or since. And with good reason, for the system is no system at all; there is neither rhyme nor reason to the choice of numbers that leads to the result. It may also be remarked that, in an open-code system, the hidden message controls the cover text, which is merely a function of the hidden plain-text. Donnelly, though he worked only on a few pages of the two parts of *Henry IV*, therefore presupposed that the magnificent language of the plays all resulted merely from the inner workings of a cipher. Did Falstaff, marvelous Falstaff, exist so exuberantly only to make sure that Bacon would have the right words for an open code? The thought is hard to bear.[3]

Although it was evident almost at once to many of Donnelly's critics—virtually all, in fact, except those who, like Donnelly, were confirmed Baconians—that the cipher was no cipher at all, nevertheless publication of the book had many results that were not unexpected. Subscriptions to the book did not sell well, and the publisher, R. S. Peale of Chicago, was not only rebuffed in his attempt to find a publishing house to distribute it in England, but it became a *cause célèbre*, resulting in newspaper debate, the publication of excerpts, and dozens of letters to the editor. The *London Strand Journal* commented in verse:

> Come from your grave, O "Bard of Avon," come,
> And tell this Yankee all his tall talks a flam,
> A figment of his too "cute brain," a hum,
> The disinterrment of his "cryptogram."[4]

In America, hostility was equally great. The *North American Review,* which had given Donnelly quasi support by publishing his article "The Shakespeare Myth" in June and July 1887, attacked him in Arthur D. Vinton's "Those Wonderful Ciphers" in the November issue. Although Vinton admitted that he had not read the book and did not intend to do so, he ridiculed as misdirected attempts to be fashionable the penchant for subscribing to anti-Shakespearean theories and searching for nonexistent ciphers.

Donnelly was also ridiculed in parody. Joseph Gilpin Pyle, a fellow Minnesotan, wrote *The Little Cryptogram*, in which, using Donnelly's method, he found a somewhat different secret in Hamlet: "*Don nill he* [Donnelly], *the author, politician, and mountebanke, will worke out the secret of this play. The Sage* [of Nininger] *is a daysie.*" The Reverend A. Nicholson, rector of St. Albans, used Donnelly's root 516 to decipher "*Master Will I am Shak'st spurre writ the play and was engaged at the Curtain.*"[5] Nicholson further extracted the same message by using Donnelly's other four root numbers.

Nevertheless, the publication of the book brought Donnelly immediate recognition of a kind he had not known before. Early in 1888 he sailed for England, where he hoped to help Peale's promotion of the book. First he went to Bacon's home at St. Albans and then to Westminster Abbey, describing both in enthusiastic detail in letters to his wife Kate, who had remained at home. Finally, however, his enthusiasm waned, as he realized that much of what he admired was the prerequisite of wealth rather than merit. "And this is the trouble with the Abbey, as it is with the world," he wrote. "Wealth (too often based on villainy) shoulders merit into a corner. Hence all that makes the Abbey respectable is condensed in what is called 'The Poets Corner.'"[6]

Nevertheless, Donnelly pursued his mission faithfully, often with the help of the wealthy whom he castigated. He lectured at Westminster Hall under the auspices of prominent Baconians before a dignified group of nine hundred—"lionized" was the word used by the American *Irish Standard* to describe his reception—and he visited the Houses of Parliament. At Lords he was the guest of the Earl of Aberdeen, an old friend but one of the wealthy, and his Farmers' Alliance temperament found the seriousness of the ritual ponderous and somewhat ridiculous.

On May 31, 1888, Donnelly defended his theories in debate before the Oxford Union, and although his reception was enthusiastic, his position was rejected by the audience by a vote of 167 to 27. Later, however, in a similar debate at Cambridge, his opponent received 120 votes to 101 for Donnelly, while nearly 300, confused, perhaps, by the complexities of Donnelly's argument, to his delight refused to vote at all.

While English Baconians were basking in the light shed by Donnelly's prominence and a number of important converts to the cause announced themselves, much of the increasingly hostile criticism in England and America became personally abusive, and Donnelly, more sensitive than in the often viciously personal political debates in backwoods Minnesota, began to strike back in the same tone.

In his diary for July 15, 1888, he commented with unaccustomed despair that "I had hoped that the ill fortune which had pursued me for twenty years—since 1868—would have lifted and left me. . . ."[7] Even his forthcoming trip to Ireland contributed to his mood:

But my book is a failure; and my political prospects are dark for there is no hope for a poor man accomplishing anything among the base and sordid politicians of Minnesota. It would seem as if my hopes rose high only to be crushed. . . . I go disheartened in the midst of wretched weather—cold, raw, and continually raining, to visit the poor oppressed, God-forsaken land of my ancestors, where the Pope has joined with the Orangemen to keep the miserable inhabitants in continued misery. . . .[8]

Donnelly still managed to enjoy his visit to Ireland and his Irish relatives, as he had a visit to Robert Burns's home in Scotland, but he was eager to return to Minnesota. However, he returned to find that sales of the book were almost nonexistent, a situation for which he blamed Peale. Eventually, suits and countersuits were brought between them, and accusations and recriminations continued, but the book was a commercial failure. Donnelly, who received a good deal of bad publicity over the controversy with Peale, eventually traded him city lots in St. Paul for the plates of the book, and the matter was ended. Donnelly thought briefly of enshrining the plates as a monument to his failure.

The book provided Donnelly with an opportunity to lecture on the Chautauqua circuit, in the fall of 1889 and later in 1891, in a series of debates with Professor J. C. Freeman. Although the experience was profitable, it was discouraging, and in 1890 he concluded that "I stand astounded before the stupidity of mankind. . . ," and wished that "there were two of me so that one could attend to politics while the other worked out the Baconian cipher."[9] Eventually he attended to both, and in 1899 published *The Cipher in the Plays and on the Tombstone.*

While *The Great Cryptogram* and its aftermath were running their course, Donnelly continued active in the Farmers' Alliance. In 1886 he recommended that the group's national program be based upon a revenue tariff, bimetalism, railroad control, and federally financed agricultural research stations, but he prevented an alliance with the

Minnesota Knights of Labor, choosing instead to forge an alliance with dissident Democrats. By default, however, a farmer-labor alliance emerged from the political warfare of that year. Without his knowledge, he was nominated for the Minnesota state legislature. Then, determined to win, he turned eagerly to the stump. He was elected in 1887 by a majority of about 800.

In the legislature he led the insurgents with a good deal of courage but with little success. When some of the labor wing of the alliance began to demand passage of a single-tax bill in the manner of Henry George, Donnelly opposed it as unwise. But his power dissipated as he turned more of his energies to finishing *The Great Cryptogram* and then turned to his trip to England.

On his return he was nominated as Farmer Labor candidate for the governorship in the fall of 1888, and, although tempted to withdraw by a Republican promise of a federal appointment, he said that his duty was in Minnesota, "defending the people from the robberies of railroad corporations." He campaigned furiously until, on October 11, convinced that the cause was futile, he withdrew from the race. But he then accepted the Democratic nomination for the legislature, losing that race in the Republican landslide by 150 votes. Nationally, Benjamin Harrison won the presidency. However, almost at once Donnelly attempted to secure election to the U.S. Senate, losing without seriously threatening either of the major party candidates. The next night he began writing a novel that, in the spirit of the age, was to predict the nature of the future. But it was neither optimistic nor utopian.

II Caesar's Column: *A Story of the Twentieth Century*

On January 19, 1889, the day after his defeat for the senate, Donnelly began to write *Caesar's Column*, which he referred to as his first and perhaps last novel. He finished it less than five months later. Submitted first to Harper and Brothers, who had published *Atlantis*, it was rejected by them, as it was by Scribner's, Houghton Mifflin, Appleton, and finally by A. C. McClurg, all of whom apparently saw the book as an incitement to revolution. Finally, however, Donnelly found a publisher in Francis J. Schulte, who had just established his own publishing house in Chicago and who agreed with Donnelly that the book did not incite the lower classes to revolution but rather warned against the excesses of revolutionary violence.

The book was finally published in April 1890, under the pseudonym Edmund Boisgilbert, M.D., in an initial edition of 2,000 copies, which rapidly sold out. In nine months it sold more than 60,000 copies in the United States alone; three editions were published in England, as were editions in Swedish, Norwegian, and, shortly thereafter, in German. When a "New Popular Edition" was published in 1906, the cover described it as including the "260th Thousand" copy of the book.

Immediately evident in *Caesar's Column* is the reason for the reluctance of publishers to issue it, even though Donnelly had already demonstrated his ability to produce a best-seller. The book reflects throughout Donnelly's sense of frustration and despair after his visit to England early in 1888 and his defeat for the senate later that year. During his English trip, after his lectures on Shakespeare and Bacon at Oxford and Cambridge, Donnelly had observed enough of English society to become convinced that true reform was impossible there or in the rest of Europe, and, after his defeat, that the same was true of America. He determined, perhaps stimulated by the success of Edward Bellamy's *Looking Backward* in 1888 (which sold more than 300,000 copies in less than two years), to tell the story of the inevitable in the form of a novel. But, whereas Bellamy's optimism resulted in a future well on the way to social justice and equality, Donnelly saw materialism, greed, and technology triumphant until the ultimate mindless revolution.

Although Donnelly, like Bellamy, was determined to describe the future, he did not, unlike other writers of reform novels, adopt Bellamy's device of putting his protagonist to sleep for a hundred years. Instead, he turned to the eighteenth century for his structural device, and cast the novel in the form of letters written home by a traveler in a foreign country. The writer is a young man named Gabriel Weltstein, and, as the book opens, he is writing to his brother Heinrich, from the modern technological wonder that is New York to their pastoral home in the State of Uganda in Africa. The young men are third-generation Swiss settlers in that land. The country that he visits is the United States, and the year is 1988, four years after George Orwell's much later *1984*, with which Donnelly's novel has a great deal in common.

The beginning, like that of Aldous Huxley's *Brave New World*, with which Donnelly's novel also merits comparison, is an immediate vision of wonder, as young Weltstein first sees the technological paradise, so different from his primitive agrarian home, that man has constructed in the New World, where presumably he has reached the highest level of civilized development. In the utopian tradition, he exclaims:

Here I am, at last, in the great city. My eyes are weary with gazing, and my mouth speechless with admiration; but in my brain rings perpetually the thought: Wonderful!—wonderful!—most wonderful!

What an infinite thing is man, as revealed in the tremendous civilization he has built up! These swarming, laborious, all-capable ants seem great enough to attack heaven itself, if they could but find a resting-place for their ladders. Who can fix a limit to the intelligence or the achievements of our species?[10]

After a momentary nostalgic glance backward at the pastoral world from which he came, Weltstein describes in great detail the wonders of the city: the first wondrous impression as his airship approached from the east: the remarkable magnetic-derived and reusable electric illumination that marks the glorious sight from afar; the wonders of the airship itself; the splendors of the magnificent hotel, suitably named the "Darwin," with its "infinite senses of cunning adjustments for the delight and gratification of the human creature" (p. 11); and finally the people who have so created this world and presumably are delighted by what they have wrought. And here, like Huxley and Orwell rather than his contemporary Bellamy, Donnelly has Weltstein notice a remarkable and frightening fact:

The chief features in the expression of the men were incredulity, unbelief, cunning, observation, heartlessness. I did not see a *good* face in the whole room: powerful faces there were, I grant you; high noses, resolute mouths, fine brows; all the marks of shrewdness and energy; a forcible and capable race; but that was all. I did not see one, my dear brother, of whom I could say, "That man would sacrifice himself for another; that man loves his fellow man." (p. 15)

From this point the flaw in the technological civilization, the flaw that results in dehumanization, becomes evident to Weltstein, and he permits his alter ego to comment on this paradox inherent in a civilization that promises so much but demands such a high price:

I could not but think how universal and irresistible must have been the influences of the age that could mold all these men and women into the same soulless likeness. I pitied them. I pitied mankind, caught in the grip of such wide-spreading tendencies. I said to myself: "Where is it all to end? What are we to expect of a race without heart or honor? What may we look for when the powers of the highest civilization supplement the instincts of tigers and wolves? Can the brain of man flourish when the heart is dead?" (pp. 15-16)

From this initial observation to the inevitable denouement to which it points, the development of the novel documents the nature of the new civilization, the paradoxes upon which it is built, and the inevitable conflict that brings it all down. For the wondrous civilization, Weltstein quickly learns, is not for all; it is only for the affluent few, those whose dehumanized faces he had observed in the hotel dining room; and the many, the masses, who have become equally dehumanized and brutalized, are in an organization known as "The Brotherhood of Terror," dedicated to destruction.

Although Donnelly had carefully denied in his preface to the novel that he was an anarchist or that he was dedicated to the overthrow of civilization, intending, rather, that the book be seen as the warning that he attempted to give, *Caesar's Column* makes evident Donnelly's conviction at the time that no warning would be heeded, that the die had already been cast, and that the revolution seen as inevitable but redeeming by Karl Marx was seen as inevitable but damning by Donnelly. The suggestion is equally clear—perhaps going back to the religious training of his youth—that man is flawed and doomed by original sin to his own destruction, as is the society that he attempts to construct.

The story continues to unfold through Weltstein's letters home, but it slips on occasion into straight narrative, as Weltstein saves an apparent beggar from assault by a coachman whose coach had run the man down. As Weltstein reverses the attack, there is a vivid foreshadowing of the bloodshed to come:

I sprang forward, and as the whip descended for a second blow I caught it, dragged it from the hand of the miscreant, and with all my power laid it over him. Each blow where it touched his flesh brought the blood, and two long red gashes appeared instantaneously upon his face. He dropped his lines and shrieked in terror. . . . (p. 21)

The beggar proves to be a well-educated young man from a good, socially conscientious family which had been victimized by the new rulers. The young man had gone underground, joined the Brotherhood, and dedicated his life to overthrowing the ruling oligarchy. Through him Weltstein meets the revolutionaries, becomes an observer of their action, and in the midst of growing violence and a new kind of brutality, he attempts, without success, to introduce a note of rationality.

In a conversation with Maximilian, the young man whom he has saved from assault and inevitable capture, Weltstein takes the opportunity to describe the perfect society as he envisions it—the logical, rational, human society that Donnelly had sought for years, a society curiously like the one called for in the Populist platform upon which Donnelly had stood so confidently a short time before: he would abolish interest; eliminate privilege established or supported by law; limit land ownership and distribute surpluses equitably; establish a paper money and demonetize gold and silver; support a technology devoted to humane human advancement; establish a rule of intellect rather than cunning; and above all, subordinate all of government to the public good. But his new friend regards him as a dreamer, one not to be taken seriously: "Let us go to dinner before you abolish all the evils of the world, or I shall be disposed to quit New York and buy a corner lot in Utopia" (p. 115), a dream society beyond man's ability to create or develop.

Paired with Weltstein's vision of Utopia is a chapter drawn largely of quotations and statistics from Donnelly's contemporaries and from magazine articles published during 1889—the *Century* of February, the *North American Review* for March, and the *Forum* for April, among others. This chapter, presented as a historical lesson given Weltstein by his new friend Maximilian, is entitled "How the World Came to Be Ruined," and again the rhetoric is to a great extent that of the campaign in which Donnelly had just participated. It describes the rise of a new plutocracy based on wealth; the corruption of the workingman by liquor interests; the difficulties on the farm; the abuses of capitalism; the rejection of such proposed solutions as Henry George's single tax. Maximilian describes the revolution at the end of the nineteenth century, the revolution foreseen by Marx but with results Marx would have denied:

In all the great cities of the world, there was a terrible outbreak of the workingmen; they destroyed much property and many lives, and held possession of the cities for several days. But the national government called for volunteers, and hundreds of thousands of warlike young men, sons of farmers, sprang to arms; and after several terrible battles, they suppressed the revolution, with the slaughter of tens of thousands of those who took part in it; while afterwards the revengeful Oligarchy sent thousands of others to the gallows. . . . The condition of the world has, however, steadily grown worse and worse. . . . (p. 96)

After these digressions Donnelly returns to the reality of 1988: a balance of terror between the armies of the Oligarchy and the underground forces of the Brotherhood, made up of the grandsons of the workers and farmers who had fought each other at the end of the nineteenth century. Whereas the Brotherhood, carefully organized to prevent betrayal or detection, largely depends upon rifles and pistols and manpower, the Oligarchy has the latest technical weapons, including a formidable force of airships, armed with bombs and poison gas and known as "The Demons."

Weltstein's education continues as first he is smuggled by Maximilian and others of the Brotherhood into a meeting of the Council of the Oligarchy and then meets the secret leadership of the Brotherhood. The former is under the leadership of Prince Cabano, a man in the long tradition of the powerful few who have exploited the many in every age; the latter is led by a giant Italian-American named Caesar Lomellini and a mysterious cripple. Both the Prince and the cripple are Jews, the former an aristocrat and the latter a nameless Russian.

Donnelly's plot carries through impassioned and eloquent but fruitless pleas by Weltstein, first to the Oligarchy and then to the Brotherhood; there are spies, counterspies, and executions; final pleas by those who propose the traditional solutions and promises of the old faiths and old virtues; and then the outbreak of war to the end, the outcome of which is determined by the defection of the pilots of the Demons to the Brotherhood as the result of a skillfully placed, timely bribe.

Again Donnelly digresses, as Maximilian takes Weltstein to a great church so that Weltstein may see for himself the failure of twentieth-century religion. The church, like the Hotel Darwin, is for the pleasure of the few, and Weltstein notes significant similarities and differences. First he sees the luxurious appointments of what is a great lecture room, and then he sees the people:

The hall was not more than half full, the greater part of those present being women. Most of them were fair and beautiful; and even those who had long passed middle age retained, by the virtue of many cunning arts, well known to these people, much of the appearance and freshness of youth. I might here note that the prolongation of life in the upper classes, and its abbreviation in the lower classes, are marked and divergent characteristics of this modern civilization. . . . The women . . . were splendid animals, and nothing more. (p. 174)

But the service itself—a song—"I could not call it a hymn; it was all about the 'Beautiful and the Good'—or something of that sort," and then a sermon—are to Weltstein confirmation of the extent to which religion in the new society has departed from the traditional. First the minister, Professor Odyard, describes developments that promise his congregation rich lives: the promise is inherent in the manipulation, for man's benefit, of the fundamental law of survival of the fittest, and the fittest in the human race are among the congregation:

What lesson does this learned and cultural age draw from these facts? Simply this: that the plan of Nature necessarily involves cruelty, suffering, injustice, destruction, death. . . .

If nature, with her interminable fecundity, pours forth millions of human beings for whom there is no place on earth, and no means of subsistence, what affair is that of ours, my brethren? We did not make them; we did not ask Nature to make them. And it is Nature's business to feed them, not yours or mine. . . .

Let us rejoice that out of the misery of the universe *we* are reserved for happiness. . . . (pp. 183–84)

As he had among the Oligarchy and the Brotherhood, Weltstein requests the right to speak, protesting, "Can you not see that Christianity was intended by God to be something better and nobler, superimposed, as an after-birth of time, on the brutality of the elder world? Does not the great doctrine of Evolution, in which you believe, preach this gospel?" (p. 188). But his protests result in a surge of brutality in the congregation, and Maximilian pulls Weltstein away, describing the imminent inevitable:

". . . The only preacher that will ever convert that congregation is Caesar Lomellini. Caesar is a bigger brute than they are—which is saying a great deal. The difference is, they are brutes who are in possession of the good things of this world; and Caesar is a brute who wants to get into possession of them. And there is another difference: they are polished and cultured brutes, and Caesar is the brute natural,—'the unaccommodated man' that Lear spoke of." (p. 190)

As the two leave the church, Donnelly introduces another digression, describing the growing love between Weltstein and the beautiful Estelle, whom he had first seen in the carriage that had nearly run down Maximilian. Estelle had been taken into the Prince's household, ostensibly, in her innocence, as a companion to a young lady who was presumably the Prince's niece but in reality his mistress, a fate also planned for Estelle. Rescued by Weltstein, she joins him in hiding with Maximilian, and their love, a love possible only to the innocent, flourishes.

Donnelly also describes the romance between Maximilian and Christina, a beautiful, talented young singer who is as innocent and good as Estelle and who had come as close as she to victimization by the exploiters. After an almost idyllic interlude as the two couples marry in a single traditional ceremony, celebrated by a simple traditional preacher, Weltstein perceives the coming cataclysm:

As I look upon it now it seems to me like one of those bright, wide rays of glorious light which we have sometimes seen bursting through a rift in the clouds, from the setting sun, and illuminating, for a brief space of time, the black, perturbed, and convulsed sky. One of our poets has compared it to—
    "A dead soldier's sword athwart his pall." But it faded, and the storm came down, at last, heavy and dark and deadly. (p. 243)

In preparation for the revolution Maximilian, still hoping that it will be a success and a new society will be created, converts all his possessions into gold, while Weltstein, with no hope for a new society, prepares for something else:

I had likewise filled one large room full of a great library of books . . . literature, science, art, encyclopedias, histories, philosophies, in fact, all the treasures of the world's genius—together with type, printing presses, telescopes, phonographs, photographic instruments, electrical apparatus, eclesions phemasticons . . . if civilization utterly perishes in the rest of the world, there, in the mountains of Africa . . . we will wait until exhausted and prostrate mankind is ready to listen to us and will help us reconstruct society upon a wise and just basis. (p. 245)

Preparations completed, one of the Demons at their disposal and one each reserved for Caesar Lomellini and the nameless second in command of the Brotherhood, there is nothing to do but wait until, in a single vivid chapter entitled "Sheal," Donnelly describes the nature of the revolution as it takes its revenge. Quickly the revolution becomes mindless, as, like its eighteenth-century predecessor, it becomes a reign of terror, violence becomes torture, and Caesar, insane with bloodletting, establishes a monument to the revolution: a huge column, filled with the bodies of the oppressors, more than a quarter of a million of them, including many whose guilt is questionable. Inscribed upon it is an epitaph written as a last ironic gesture by Weltstein:

This Great Monument
is
Erected by
Caesar Lomellini,
Commanding General of
The Brotherhood of Destruction,
in
commemoration of
The Death and Burial of
Modern Civilization   (p. 282)

Then follows a list of the crimes of the members of the Oligarchy, much like the list of crimes attributed to George III by Thomas Jefferson in the Declaration of Independence. But whereas the crimes Jefferson ascribed to the King were essentially violations of human rights, of the natural rights of the eighteenth century, these were crimes against God and Man: "They drove justice from the land and installed cruelty, ignorance, despair and vice in its place. . . . They degraded humanity and outraged God. . . . From this ghastly pile let it derive the great lesson, that no earthly government can endure which is not built on mercy, justice, truth and love" (pp. 282–83).

Maximilian's final efforts to restore order are failures; Caesar, in Prince Cabano's palace, institutes a reign of drunken carnival; the nameless Jew flees with $100 million to set up a new Jerusalem; and there is nothing for Maximilian, Weltstein, and their few followers to do but flee, set up a tiny Utopia based upon justice and sound populist economics, and wait until they can teach mankind the lessons that have thus far eluded them. As they look back, Maximilian reflects upon what revolution has taught him:

Ignorance, passion, suspicion, brutality, criminality, will be the lions in the path. Men who have such dreadful memories of labor can scarcely be forced back into it. And who is to employ them? After about three-fourths of the human family have died of hunger, or been killed, the remainder, constituting, by the law of the survival of the fittest, the most powerful and brutal, will find it necessary, for self-defense against each other, to form squads or gangs. The greatest fighter in each of these will become chief, as among all savages. Then the history of the world will be slowly repeated. A bold ruffian will conquer a number of the adjacent squads, and become a king. Gradually, and in its rudest forms, labor will begin again; at first exercised principally by slaves. Men will exchange liberty for protection. After a century or two a kind of commerce may arise. Then will follow other centuries of wars, between provinces or nations. A new aristocracy will spring up. Culture will lift its head. A great power, like Rome in the old world, may arise. Some vast superstition may take possession of the world; and Alfred, Victoria and Washington may be worshipped, as Saturn, Juno and Hercules were in the past; with perhaps dreadful and bloody rights like those of the Carthaginians and ancient Mexicans. And so, step by step, mankind will reenact the great human drama, which begins always with a tragedy, runs through a comedy, and terminates in a catastrophe. (p. 291)

Contrasted with this picture of cataclysm, slow social evolution through chaos to violence to an order imposed by force—a story that Donnelly had suggested in the society described in *Atlantis*, a social cataclysm in degree not unlike that which shook the physical earth in

Ragnarok—is the small new society, an agrarian paradise, established in the remoteness of Africa. Privilege is abolished, as is interest; gold and silver are demonetized; state ownership eliminates abuse of utilities, railroads, and mines; checks, balance, and the people provide for secure, orderly government; the conditions of employment are matters of public concern. None of this is impossible or visionary, Donnelly concludes:

> There is no reason why the ingenuity of man should not be applied to these great questions. It has conquered the forces of steam and electricity, but it has neglected the great adjustments of society, on which the happiness of millions depends. If the same intelligence which has been bestowed on perfecting the steam-engine had been directed to a consideration of the correlations of man to man, and pursuit to pursuit, supply and demand would have precisely matched each other, and there need have been no pauperism in the world— save that of the sick and imbecile. And the very mendicants would begin to rise when the superincumbent pressure of those who live on the edge of pauperism had been withdrawn. (p. 307)

The novel ends on a note of hope, even of optimism, not evident in the rest of the novel, and Donnelly's purpose is clear: to present a picture of horrible, inevitable destruction. The scene of the drunken Caesar demanding that more be killed so that the column may be built higher is, with Faulkner's description of the rape of Temple Drake by Popeye, one of the truly horrible scenes in American fiction. Donnelly's purpose is to convince the potential victims and killers in such a cataclysm, the industrialists and bankers and their supporters on one hand and those who preach revolution on the other, to recognize the inevitability of the collision and its aftermath. Their intelligence and self-interest if not humanitarianism will then prevail, and they will take the path of justice so clearly pointed out to them by Donnelly in this novel as well as by him and his fellow Populists in political campaigns past and to come. If this recognition does take place, the course of life will be drastically changed: "And so mankind moves with linked hands through happy lives to deaths; and God smiles down upon them from his throne beyond the stars" (p. 313).

Caesar's Column is not, by any critical standards, a good novel; it has too many of the flaws shared by too much of the bad literature of its time to ascribe to it any permanent place in American belletristic history. As hurriedly written and lacking in smoothness or credibility as any of the pulp works of fiction then beginning their domination of the American subliterary scene, *Caesar's Column* is as melodramatic as *The Count of Monte Cristo*, then touring the country in the version starring James O'Neill and, together with the book, perhaps part of Donnelly's limited contact with the contemporary world of letters then available even to the Sage of Nininger. As Walter Rideout points out, Donnelly would probably have had access to the Dumas novel in translation in either the 1888 or the 1889 edition. *Cristo* and *Caesar's Column* share the name Maximilian for a leading character.

Structure is equally faulty, with too many digressions intended to prolong the reader's excitement as well as to provide didactic statements by juxtaposition of competing points of view. Clichés abound, and the speeches reflect the nineteenth-century political tradition of which Donnelly had for so long been a part—emotional, flowery, and sonorous—all techniques undoubtedly useful on a stump not yet graced by electronic amplification but tedious at best on the printed page, particularly as their digressions interfere in the flow of an exciting narrative.

In its melodramatic way, *Caesar's Column* is as exciting as Donnelly intended it to be, as the world of 1988 rushes to its destruction, but virtue—the very little virtue still existent in that world—is saved, Atlantis-like, to preserve the spark of civilization that will stimulate other men in other times. Weltstein's rescue of his loved one, significantly a collateral descendant of George Washington, from the monster-Prince is clear evidence that the good in modern civilization, preserved by Weltstein to be carried back to Uganda, will survive and flourish in the true Utopia they establish there.

But the true merits of the book are other than literary: it provides a remarkable insight into Donnelly's vision of his own time and the course of the future; it provides insights into a variety of his attitudes toward contemporary peoples, institutions, and values; and it offers a remarkable example of the curious pessimism that marked so much of the reform impulse, particularly in literature, during the last decade of the nineteenth century and the first of the twentieth.

Perhaps the most significant element in the book is the relentlessness of Donnelly's attack on those who reject the traditional humane values of reform or of Christian charity. This attack is best exemplified in his portrayal of the kind of Social Darwinism preached by William Summer, Russell Conwell, and others who insisted that Darwin's concept of the survival of the fittest in the biological world be extended to the economic and social realms and, indeed, even to the theological. Here, in spite of his long-lapsed Catholicism, Donnelly returns to the rhetoric of fundamental

Christianity as he calls for Christ to drive, once more, moneychangers from the temple:

... He who drove the money-changers out of the temple, and denounced the aristocrats of his own country as whited sepulchres, and preached a communism of goods, would not view to-day with patience or equanimity the dreadful sufferings of mankind. . . . Oh! for the quick-pulsing, warm-beating, mighty human heart of the man of Galilee! Oh! for his uplifted hand, armed with a whip of scorpions, to depopulate the temples of the world, and lash his recreant preachers into devotion to the cause of his poor afflicted children! (p. 169)

But Donnelly's rhetoric is neither a plea nor a prayer; it is, rather, a regret that Christ's appearance is not forthcoming, that the only reality is the inevitability of cataclysm, that only in the never-never land of Uganda, in a simple, uncomplicated agrarian garden—a garden accepting modern technology but rejecting the kind of control that had brought it into existence—can cataclysm be avoided. But it can be avoided only as long as virtue reigns, "And the wolves have disappeared; and our little world is a garden of peace and beauty, musical with laughter" (p. 313). And this vision, too, seems neither plea nor prayer, but regret that this garden is as far beyond the reach of the exploited as it is beyond the imagination or vision of the exploiters.

Perhaps most evident in the novel is Donnelly's lack of faith in man's ability to control what he has created, to permit whatever good impulses he may have to direct his actions, or to control his destiny. Rather, like the vision of reality created by Theodore Dreiser, a younger contemporary then serving the apprenticeship from which *Sister Carrie* was to emerge little more than a decade later, Donnelly shows man as selfish, weak, and stupid, the creature of forces beyond his control, indeed beyond his comprehension. But whereas Dreiser's pessimism was cosmic, rooted in the impersonality of a mindless, whimsical fate, Donnelly's is that of the frustrated idealist whose impulses remain strong but who finds himself unable to translate them into meaningful, purposeful action. Like Weltstein, Donnelly can only cry out the truth, knowing at the same time that he will be neither heard nor understood. Donnelly's vision of the technological paradise of 1988 is descended directly from Herman Melville's "Paradise of Bachelors and Tartarus of Maids" in its recognition of the sterility and dehumanization inherent in such a society, and it points the way toward Aldous Huxley's *Brave New World* and

George Orwell's *1984* as it makes clear the ultimate antihuman impulse of the machine society. But none of the others sees, as does Donnelly, that supreme moment when technology run rampant, captured and unleashed by its servants, makes the nightmare real.

Donnelly's portrayals of Prince Cabano and the nameless second-in-command of the Brotherhood as Jews have resulted in perennial charges of anti-Semitism against him and are seen as evidence of a racism—indeed a rustic incipient fascism—inherent in populism, and this charge persists in spite of evidence in the text and out of it to refute it. These portrayals are rather part of the pattern of cyclical emergence, growth, and decay that Donnelly sees as the nature of civilizations from the days of Atlantis to our own day and beyond. Prince Cabano—an aristocrat rather than a simple carpenter—is the last symbolic and actual ruler of a cycle that had begun in Judea two millennia before, and the nameless renegade escapes to Jerusalem in a mad effort to begin the same pattern once more, a pattern fore-doomed in its dependence upon money rather than ideology or idealism for its foundation. The role of the Jew as the founder of the age-old tradition of which we are the heirs is paralleled by the perverted role of the Jew in the destruction of that tradition, and one more phase of the human story has come full circle, further evidence of the natural rythmic pattern that Donnelly had perceived in nature and civilizations. Here he demonstrates that the cycle is a law of social existence as surely as he had portrayed it as a law of nature in *Atlantis* and *Ragnarok*.

Caesar's Column is Donnelly's most eloquent expression of man's fate, his vision of a future that was perhaps, by the last decade of the nineteenth century, already inevitable, and his projection of a curious, largely unimaginative future: the skies crowded with airships and the cities crowded with horses and carriages; technical mastery and moral bankruptcy; clear warnings, yet a lemminglike search for self-destruction. But Weltstein and Maximilian live because technology makes their survival possible, and the idyllic retreat provides hope for the future. Yet what one carries from the book is not the freshness and brightness of that last image, and Donnelly must have known it; what one remembers is the sheer horror of *Caesar's Column* and the madness of the liberator as his debauchery outreaches anything Prince Cabano might have attempted in his most jaded, sated, demanding moments. Donnelly contrasts two images, and the vision of despair and horror is by far the more compelling.

While Donnelly was writing *Caesar's Column*, his political for-

tunes were ebbing, but on March 4, 1890, he served as keynote
speaker for the Minnesota convention of the Northwest Alliance.
Although he pleased the audience by his wit and his barbed
comments on the political realities of Minnesota, he did not capture
the alliance presidency. That summer he was also defeated in his bid
for the gubernatorial nomination, but he did succeed in securing an
Alliance Labor Union nomination for the state senate. In a major
Republican upset that fall, Donnelly, to his own surprise as well as
that of a good many professionals, was elected. Almost immediately
he began to play a role in the national leadership of the alliance.

CHAPTER 5

The Miraculous and the Mundane

D URING the fall of 1890 Donnelly fought, sometimes separately but often collectively, Democrats, Republicans, and the leadership of his own alliance. In each case the substance of his position was the same: the need for reform in the parties and the denunciation of those who had made alliances with the exploiters. As the author of *Caesar's Column* he had achieved a substantial amount of notoriety among national reform leaders, and he, in turn, began to think again of a national role for himself.

In the Minnesota legislature Donnelly supported his usual reform interests—railroad control and tax—supported agricultural experimentation, and added to them the abolition of child labor and the introduction of the Australian ballot. He commented, however, that he was "thwarted by the fools and the knaves:—and in public affairs it is hard to know which is most dangerous to society."[1]

Nevertheless, while Donnelly fought and lost his battles in the legislature and within the Alliance Labor party, he became increasingly popular on the national reform scene. Not only was he praised as the author of *Caesar's Column*, but in the South he was spoken of as a potential Presidential candidate of a projected third party. As the convention of reform parties and groups, scheduled for Cincinnati in May 1891, came nearer, Donnelly was spoken of as a natural leader. He became chairman of the convention's resolutions committee, the group most instrumental in making possible the convention in St. Louis in February 1892, which brought the Populist party into existence. Donnelly, the hero at Cincinnati, had achieved the national momentum toward reform and the high political office that he had sought for nearly forty years. And he had another reform novel in press.

I Doctor Huguet

Written during the fall of 1890, while Donnelly was engaged in the bitter campaign of that year, *Doctor Huguet* is, like *Caesar's*

Column, a shocker, and like its predecessor it depends to a great extent on horror for its impact as it attacks moral and social duplicity. Unlike *Caesar's Column*, however, it makes no attempt to be prophetic, and maintains itself entirely on the level of fantasy.

The story concerns a brilliant young Southern white liberal physician, a radical supporter of racial equality in a South rapidly stratifying into segregation a generation after the Civil War. Donnelly's science permits the exchange of Huguet's mind and soul with those of a brutalized young black. As a result the substance of *Doctor Huguet* is more daring than any other novel of its age. Donnelly felt strongly that only a nightmare could adequately reflect the quality of life experienced by the oppressed in such a society, and this nightmare is reflected throughout a book that, in spite of a good many flaws, is a powerful polemic. Even yet it remains a powerful indictment of a system based upon injustice and dedicated to a process of dehumanization.

Like *Caesar's Column*, *Doctor Huguet* is a first-person narrative, but the narrator is not an observer-participant as was Gabriel Weltstein. He is the central character, who begins the novel with what are perhaps the most arresting opening lines since Edgar Allan Poe's "The Masque of the Red Death," a work and an author at least superficially related to the undercurrents of horror that run through *Caesar's Column*, occasionally breaking the surface in that work and emerging as the main stream of *Doctor Huguet*. Just as Poe in 1842 wrote, "The 'Red Death' had long devastated the country. No pestilence had ever been so fatal, or so hideous. Blood was its avatar and seal . . . ," Donnelly begins with a line as suggestive of horror, but his is more clearly defined in human terms: "I have made up my mind to tell the whole dreadful story, let the consequences be what they may."[2] But whereas Poe's purpose is to engender an emotional response in his reader, Donnelly's is to make evident to him a truth at once moral and social:

But it seems to me that I have been chosen, by some extra-mundane, superhuman intelligence, out of the multitude of mankind, and subjected to a terrible and unparalleled experience, in order that a great lesson may be taught to the world; and that it is a duty, therefore, which I owe to the world, and which I must not shrink from or avoid, to make known all the facts of that existence, at whatever cost of shame or agony to myself. . . . Those whom God so honors he agonizes. (pp. 7–8)

With this suggestion that if the poor are blessed by God even while they suffer the prophet is liable to greater honor and suffering,

Donnelly's narrator hero sets the stage for the horror and moral to follow. Huguet is "an aristocrat of aristocrats." His home is an heirloom and a work of art as well as the stereotype of a Southern antebellum pastoral paradise; he has plenty of money with which to indulge himself; and, like so many other wealthy Americans who would otherwise be idle, he is urged to run for public office, a commonplace occurrence that, Donnelly indicates, is perhaps as often the result of greed as of ambition, talent, or interest on the part of the potential political leader:

If he has not himself any predisposition in that direction, he will be sought out by the professional politicians and forced into such a career—not, it may be, from any admiration of his talents, for he may perchance, possess none; but from a desire to get their hands into his "barrel," as it is called in the vernacular of the day, or into his "pocket," as our ancestors would have said. The advance of the world is shown in the fact that the "pocket" has grown into a "barrel." Civilization enlarges everything, even corruption. (p. 11)

Huguet, however, has not been touched by that corruption, largely because he had no ambition and was well aware of the nature of public office, "discredited if not dishonored, by the kind of men who ruled it" (p. 11). Instead, Huguet turns to his library, to "communion with the mighty souls of the past," and ultimately to love, a love which, however, Huguet knows rationally is merely "a primal instinct imposed on humanity for the perpetuation of the race." The object of his passion is Mary Ruddeman, daughter of a Southern family as stereotyped as Huguet's mansion. But Huguet's scientific knowledge has taught him that she is different. As a result of the "law of variation," Donnelly's version of the mechanism of evolution, Mary Ruddeman is a *freak*:

True, she had inherited all the courage, daring, high-spirited and honorable impulses of her parents and ancestors; it would be impossible for her to commit a debased or degrading act. But she was something that none of her predecessors had ever been. There were plenty of intelligent Ruddemans; but Mary was the first of her race that was *intellectual. . . .* (p. 14)

The attraction between the two is inevitable, according to Donnelly's science, and it is mutual, as their discussions lead them to agreement on the nature and meaning of the great books of the past and to an awareness of the nature of abstract justice and its lack in the world. Eventually they are led to love. Concurrently, Mary's ambition tempts Huguet to seek a future in politics, a career worthy of him, and, Donnelly asserts, a preoccupation that is instinctive to the Southern mind.

Huguet's courtship of Mary and his growing acquaintanceship with her father and their neighbors give Donnelly opportunity to discourse upon his—and his narrator's—views on the equality and origin of races, the nature of the ultimate reality, and the impact of environment, disease, and nutrition upon human development. In an exchange among Huguet, Colonel Ruddeman, Major McFettridge ("who was something of a radical" [p. 52]), and Lawyer Buryhill (a Northerner "who had a smattering of scientific knowledge" [p. 53], but "was more Southern than Southerners in his intolerance of the blacks" [p. 54]), Donnelly has his narrator range widely over the intellectual and social issues of his day, in each case defining the truth as Donnelly insists it must be. On the nature of man, Donnelly is clear:

"Why, surely, said the Colonel, "the principles that apply to white men do not reach those wretched creatures; they are hardly human."

"Simian," said Lawyer Buryhill. . . .

"They prove the truth of Darwinism," added Major Berrisford; "they are one of the links that bind our own race to the animal creation."

"No, no, gentlemen," I replied; "do not be unfair to them: a race that could produce a Toussaint L'Ouverture is not simian. You cannot rank a coal-black negro, like Toussaint—who compelled the surrender of a French army under Brandicourt; took twenty-eight Spanish batteries in four days; and, with half their force, compelled the surrender of an English army—with the monkeys. He brought Napoleon's brother-in-law, Leclerc, to his knees, and was only overcome at last by treachery. . . . (pp. 53–54)

Unwilling to accept Huguet's evidence, Buryhill, speaking for the prejudice of his age, prepares the way for a discussion not only of the nature of man but of the relationships among the races of men and between man and God. Buryhill questions Huguet:

"But will you not admit . . . that the negro stands nearer to the brute world than all other races?"

"No," I said; "I do not admit it. But even if it were true, there is a vast, an impassable gulf between the lowest man and the highest ape; a gap which only the creative presence of the great God, with vast designs for the human race, could fill. And, if the taint of the brute adheres to the negro, does it not cling to us all? . . . What right have we to question God—the recipients of whose bounty we are, for life itself and all its blessings—and ask Him why He sees fit to put other men on this planet, and paint their skin a different color from our own? . . ." (pp. 54–55)

From this point, Donnelly digresses, as he often does in such discussions, to a refutation of the nature of God as defined by the post-Darwinism naturalists, as he has Huguet define God in terms reminiscent of Thomas Paine in *The Age of Reason*:

"Oh," said Buryhill, with a sneer. . . , "the best intelligences are now agreed that belief in God is one of the fables of the world's youth; and that there is nothing in the universe but this self-acting, self-perpetuating thing we call Nature."

. . . "Indeed! why, you use the very intelligence which God has given you to deny that there is a great Intelligence in the universe. You conceive of a great work-shop without a master mechanic. You perceive a million delicate adjustments in nature, and you conclude that those adjustments adjusted themselves. You would have design, but no designer. . . . It is impossible to conceive a vast creation without a general intelligence; a creation possessing only spots of unconnected intelligence, scattered here and there, self-born, self-luminous, and mortal." (pp. 55–56)

If the concept of God that Donnelly ascribes approvingly to Huguet sounds curiously like that of the enlightened thinking of Thomas Paine in the eighteenth century, the concept of human equality that Huguet expresses is much like Abraham Lincoln's reply to Stephen A. Douglas on August 21, 1858. Donnelly writes, in terms typical of much of the advanced thinking of the late nineteenth century:

"I do not say what the black race may come to be in time, under favorable conditions, but at present I must admit that they are an inferior people. It must be remembered, however, that for countless generations they have occupied the most malarial and unhealthy lands in the world—lands in which no white child can pass the age of puberty, in which no white adult's life is worth a year's purchase. . . ." (pp. 56–57)

For this and other similar statements Donnelly has been called a racist by recent scholars and critics, just as Lincoln has been called racist by the revisionists for saying that "he [the Negro] is not my equal in many respects—certainly not in color, perhaps not in moral or intellectual endowment. . . ."[3] But in each case the revisionist ignores the significant context out of which the evidence comes. In Lincoln's case it was the remark that followed, the insistence that "in the right to eat the bread, without leave of anybody else, which his own hand earns, *he is my equal and the equal of Judge Douglas, and the equal of every living man*."[4] Donnelly, through Huguet, expresses a similar conviction:

"And do you think," said Buryhill, with his nose in the air, and a frown on his brow, "that the negroes should have the same political rights as the whites?"

I was aware that I was advancing upon ticklish ground, but I could not get clear of my logical faculty, and so I replied:

"Why not? Political equality does not imply social equality, or physical equality, or moral equality, or race equality. When you go to the ballot-box to vote you find a group assembled of white men, originally of different nationalities—Yankee, French, German, Irish, Scotch—of different complexions, conditions, mental powers, education and knowledge. No two are alike; no two are equal in any respect, and yet they all peacefully unite in expressing their political preferences. The right to participate in the government, in a republic, is like the right to breathe the atmosphere. . . . Because a man votes beside me at the polling-place, it does not follow that I must take him into my house, or wed him to my daughter, any more than those results follow because we breathe the same air." (pp. 60–61)

In making clear all of these positions, it is obvious that Huguet is speaking for Donnelly, and it appears that the chapter in which they appear, Chapter VIII, "The Debate," the longest in the book, is largely digression. But as the novel progresses it becomes evident that what appears to be didactic digression is intrinsically part of character development and plot advancement. Not only is Huguet's liberal position on issues of the time and place made clear, but there is a good deal of foreshadowing of plot development as the character traits of others are made clear: Buryhill is a bigot, intellectually dishonest, and potentially a scoundrel; Colonel Ruddeman is gentle, sympathetic, and troubled, a product of his time and place, but a man whose mind is as open as his home; Major McFettridge is rational and fair-minded. And Mary, who overhears and is afraid for the effects of Huguet's views on his potential political career, is troubled. Rational rather than bigoted, however, her fear is that Huguet's views will make him ineffective:

. . . "You would destroy yourself and all your future capacity for usefulness. You would be hated, despised, persecuted; your utterances would be distorted, exaggerated; you would be regarded as a demagogue or a lunatic."

"But," I said, "some one must die for the truth. . . ."

". . .Remember this is a *race* conflict, and the contentions of races with one another are always more bitter than the battles of rival religions, for every physical attribute which separates the combatants accentuates the ferocity of the struggle. . . . One must go, right or wrong, with his class."

". . .Almost thou persuadest me to be a—hypocrite!"

"No, no," she said, earnestly, "not a hypocrite, but a statesman. A true statesman is one who adapts righteousness to circumstances; as the Swiss peasant builds his house, irregularly it may be, but strongly, against the crooked inequalities of the mountain. He could not erect a symmetrical Greek temple upon the face of the precipice, but he secures a humble home, where love and peace may find shelter in the midst of Alpine tempests." (pp. 73–75)

Huguet resists her argument, protesting at length, and, even as she admits the justice of his position, she nevertheless continues to reject its wisdom and to assert her own. Finally, however, persuaded not by her logic, but by his love for her, "I took her hand, I yielded. I promised to abandon my convictions and throw the weight of my station and my intelligence against the poor wretches who were already borne down to the earth by the accumulated weight of their misfortunes" (p. 81).

As the chapter "The Temptation" and its ultimate surrender, not unlike its biblical parallel leading to man's fall, conclude, Donnelly has at the same time concluded his definition of the lot of the Negro in the last decade of the nineteenth century. The black man in America, caught up in the realities, the pragmatic decisions, and the pseudo-scientific arguments of the age, his rights compromised away by political considerations, and himself finally condemned to an inferior position by a Supreme Court that permitted a euphemistic separate but equal existence, had, by the time Donnelly wrote, become virtually invisible, even to all too many of Donnelly's contemporaries who, like Huguet, for whatever reason, had surrendered the conviction of their consciences for convenience and other considerations.

The book might have ended at this point, essentially a thinly fictionalized polemic, but Donnelly's concern with the wondrous, with that dimension of life that transcends the limitations of human experience, uses this initial delineation of ideas and positions as preface to the rapid development of a story of horror. Based upon the unexplainable, unlike the simple coincidence of a missent letter or mistaken identities that has provided the impetus for works as diverse as Shakespeare's plays and O. Henry's short stories, *Dr. Huguet* from this point moves with the massive, humanly incomprehensible certainty of *Atlantis* or *Ragnarok* toward a crisis as inescapable as those cataclysms. Donnelly manages this move through the introduction of a being he was to use again later in *The Golden Bottle*: the sudden apparition of Christ as the dispenser of justice, in this case of punishment, just as in the later novel He was to bring economic equality. As Huguet wakes from his sleep that night, or perhaps continues to dream, the vision appears, a vision that Huguet recognizes at once, and it speaks: "'These, too, are my children. For them, also I died on the cross!'" (p. 86).

In his fear as the vision fades, Huguet pleads with God for

forgiveness and understanding of the vision, yet the image remains with him:

What did it mean? The Christ surrounded by millions of dark hands. Why *dark* hands? Where were the hands of my own race? And why did this vision come to *me*? What had I to do with the negroes? Could it mean that I had been false, in my heart, to God and my fellow-man? (p. 87)

Its meaning becomes evident when, after a fitful sleep, Huguet wakes to find himself black, to find that, although his mind remains unchanged, his body has been exchanged for that of a Negro, one Sam Johnsing, a perennial chicken thief, drunk, and ne'er-do-well. Huguet's bewilderment changes to rage and then madness as he strikes down the Negro woman—Johnsing's wife—in front of him and rushes out of the Negro shack in which he finds himself:

I ran wildly along the open road, dimly lighted by the stars, past numerous, closely-clustered negro cabins. It was the dead of night, and no one was abroad. I ran and ran, as if I would run away from this hated body which enclosed me. Now and then I stopped, as the thought recurred to me, "It is all a horrible dream; it cannot be true. I shall waken soon!" No, no. I examined again and again my arms, hands, limbs. *I was a negro.* I leaped up in the air as if I would spring out of myself. I rolled in the dust. I shrieked; I cried. Then I prayed. Down on my knees—down on my very face, I prostrated myself, and cried out, in the midst of the silent night, to the merciful God to spare me and lift this curse from me. (p. 93)

As impossible as the fact seems, Huguet is forced to accept it. Not only does his assertion that he is indeed Dr. Huguet receive nothing but laughter, but he begins almost immediately to suffer the degradation that dehumanizes: arrest without cause, harsh treatment, even arrest for the theft of his own thought. But gradually things change. First, Negroes, particularly his own servant Ben, and Abigail, the near-white servant of the Ruddemans, recognize his true identity. Others see him as Voodoo, or bewitched at first, but then gradually recognize him. Finally, even Mary perceives the truth of his identity, but that truth is apparently forever altered by the fact of his color. His encounter with her nearly leads to his death, as white men see only a black man accosting a white woman. Only Abigail's and Mary's quick wits save him.

Huguet's attempts to find work for which he is suited—teaching at two schools and even clerkships—are frustrated by his color, while Sam Johnsing, with Huguet's identity and his fortune, sinks into debauchery. Huguet then establishes a school for the area's blacks, and he is able to frustrate Buryhill's attempts to defraud Colonel Ruddeman. The extent of the cruel reverse is finally acknowledged, but it seems final. At last, however, Huguet is resigned:

I was happy—happy to find that at last, despite my black skin, my active brain could work effectively, and I could achieve something. The sense of power returned to me, and I found myself singing, for the first time since the night of my dreadful transformation. (p. 236)

The nocturnal visits to Huguet continue, however; first there is a band of white-masked white men, who beat him nearly to death, and then there is another, one he had perceived before, and which he recognizes at once:

THE FACE OF CHRIST
That unutterable, that indescribable face! But the threat had gone out of the great thoughtful, pitiful eyes; and the mouth, the sweet mouth, smiled upon me. Yes! Blessed be God! It smiled upon me! Upon me, the most wretched of men; the poor, unhappy, broken-hearted negro. And then a dark shadow . . . crept around the luminous head, and the shadow grew and expanded, not suppressing the light, but filled with the light, and yet a darkness painted on the light; and still it grew until it spread far beyond the narrow boundaries of my chamber into infinitude; and then it began to resolve itself into small forms—into millions of faces—faces brown, yellow, pale, black, but none of them white; faces of men, women, and children; of the young and the old; of the gray-haired grandsire and the little infant—millions upon millions of faces—and every face looked into mine and smiled upon me!
And the great eyes glanced around at the innumerable multitude, and said:
"WHOSOEVER DEALETH MERCIFULLY WITH THE LEAST OF THESE IS NUMBERED AMONG THE BELOVED OF GOD." (pp. 283–84)

The vision fades, and Huguet knows that his deliverance is near; only its manner remains a mystery, and, convinced that it can only be death, he determines to do to the end what has become his duty: teaching the blacks to live in a hostile society. To both blacks and whites he preaches mercy and justice; to the blacks, Huguet advises the break-up of the black allegiance to a single party—obviously the Republican, to most blacks not the party that had abandoned them in 1876 but that which had freed them in 1865, although Huguet does not name it. Instead he counsels, obviously reflecting the recent Populist attempt to unite black farmers with white, that they seek to join "a vast army, with principles for banners and ballots for weapons" (p. 289), the party that sought economic freedom and brotherhood for all men.
Before he finishes, however, the final horror, that peculiar to black

existence in a white South, is thrust upon him. A white-masked mob attacks the schoolhouse, blacks are slaughtered, and Huguet is hanged from a convenient limb, his body the target for the mob's bullets. In the final instant the caricature of Huguet, the black Sam Johnsing in Huguet's body, fires a pistol and the bullet strikes the swinging body. At that same moment a woman darts out of the crowd and stabs the false Huguet. As in the execution in Ambrose Bierce's "An Occurrence at Owl Creek Bridge," it is the end.

But again, as in Bierce's story, it is not. Huguet revives, sorely wounded, but alive. And it is no fantasy in the last moment of life, but reality. Suddenly wrongs are righted, Sam Johnsing is dead, and although the faithful servants Ben and Abigail are also killed, peace is restored, and justice is done. Once more united, Mary and Huguet are determined to spend their lives preaching and working for justice.

Although the novel ends with a sudden surge of optimism and promise of justice, qualities only incidentally present in *Caesar's Column*, the two novels are technically quite similar. Each is, like Donnelly's first two pseudoscientific works, the study of a cataclysm, carefully documented. In *Atlantis* and *Ragnarok* the cataclysm is natural and physical; in the two novels it is social and psychological. Of the novels, that in *Caesar's Column* leaves the reader with almost no hope, while that in *Dr. Huguet* permits a good deal. In each case, however, the attitude at the end is the result of Donnelly's purpose. In the former novel, he is presenting a warning, a vision of the future if man refuses to seek justice and in the process insures his own brutalization and death; in the latter, he portrays the promise inherent in man's willingness to do the right thing because it is right.

Nevertheless, Donnelly's technique of the cataclysm, however suitable it may be for his scientific theories, contributes little to the effectiveness of a work of fiction, whether conceived as a work of literary art or as the vehicle for a tract. However successful *Doctor Huguet* may have been in sales—it went through five apparently small editions—its critics perceived its artistic failure immediately. The reviewer for the *New York Sun* wrote:

There is no objection to a Sunday School tract on the duty of civilized men to the colored races, but there is no justification for illustrating this duty by the crude device of transforming a South Carolina gentleman and scholar into a negro chicken thief, transferring their souls to each other's body, and interspersing this magic with miraculous visions of Christ. Such a story is not likely to be read out of the nursery except under compulsion, and even in the nursery it would be demoralizing.[5]

In its fantasy, its moralizing, and its obvious sentimentality, the novel certainly might be considered demoralizing in the decade that saw constitutional sanction given institutionalized segregation, grandfather clauses, and lynch law. In the tradition of the great antislavery tracts of the pre–Civil War years, most notably Harriet Beecher Stowe's *Uncle Tom's Cabin*, it is a powerful polemic directed at institutionalized evil, certainly not that of the nursery, but more properly of the courtroom and the legislative chamber. Donnelly clearly identifies the race issue, imposed upon blacks and whites alike by the ruling classes, as a means for maintaining control, if necessary by white-masked riders in the night. *Doctor Huguet* is a powerful argument in favor of the means by which the people might gain the power which is rightfully theirs.

At the heart of the book is Donnelly's compassion for the downtrodden, a sympathy and support to which he had given voice numerous times in the past. At the end of *Doctor Huguet* he writes, "The great Gospel of Brotherly Love is the true solvent in which must melt away forever the hates of races and the contention of castes" (p. 309), an echo of his assertion on the floor of the House of Representatives twenty-five years before:

The earth is God's, and all the children of God have an equal right upon its surface; and human legislation which would seek to subvert this truth merely legislates injustice into law; and he who believes that injustice conserves the peace, order, and welfare of society has read history to little purpose.[6]

If Donnelly's sentiments in 1867 found a great deal of support in the ranks of Radical Republicans in 1867, they found very little, even from his own radical supporters and colleagues, a quarter-century later. *Doctor Huguet* was addressed to those who had read even their own history to little purpose; unfortunately, it had little effect.

Nevertheless, there were some who understood his purpose and appreciated his efforts. In the Donnelly Papers at the Minnesota Historical Society there are letters from Burton O. Aylesworth, President of Drake University, who wrote that the work "assaults prejudice like a tempest. . . ," and from Dr. J. H. Smith, a black physician, who wrote, "Any white man who can afford to speak out in such unmistakable terms for a race who have so little with which to reward him, is to be praised by every colored man." But the great American majority, to whom the book was addressed, neither heard nor replied.

II   *The St. Louis Convention*

While *Doctor Huguet* ran its course, Donnelly was too involved in the lawsuits his political activities had engendered and with his movement into national leadership of the emerging third party to be depressed at the book's lack of success. On February 22, 1892, he was in St. Louis for the great convention. He made one of the opening speeches, and upon his motion delegates from the Women's Christian Temperance Union, including Frances Willard herself, were seated.

Out of the St. Louis convention the coalition that was the People's party emerged. In introducing the party platform preamble, Donnelly was both eloquent and convincing as he defined the crisis out of which the party was born:

We meet in the midst of a nation brought to the verge of moral, political and material ruin. Corruption dominates the ballot box, the legislatures, the Congress, and touches even the ermine of the bench. The people are demoralized. Many of the States have been compelled to isolate the voters at the polling places in order to prevent universal intimidation or bribery. The newspapers are subsidized or muzzled; public opinion silenced; business prostrate, our homes covered with mortgages, labor impoverished, and the land concentrating in the hands of capitalists. The urban workmen are denied the right of organization for self-protection; imported pauperized labor beats down their wages; a hireling standing army, unrecognized by our laws, is established to shoot them down, and they are rapidly disintegrating to European conditions. . . .[7]

Donnelly's preamble makes it evident that he has the great precedents of the Declaration of Independence and the Constitution before him. The platform he has prepared to present to the convention is indeed a renewal of those two documents, a declaration of freedom from the abuses of the present, and a Bill of Rights to prevent the resurgence of abuses in the future. He concludes:

In order to restrain the extortions of aggregated capital, to drive the money changers out of the temple, "to form a [more] perfect union, to establish justice, insure domestic tranquility, provide for the common defense, promote the general welfare and secure the blessings of liberty for ourselves and our posterity," we do ordain and establish the following platform.[8]

The platform itself is anticlimactic, shorter than its preamble. Donnelly was repeatedly cheered, the preamble and platform, twin keys to founding the new party, adopted, and the convention adjourned, to meet again at Omaha for the purpose of nominating candidates for national office.

At home Donnelly was instrumental in constructing a People's party of Minnesota by persuading local chapters to ratify the St. Louis preamble and platform. Although Jerry Simpson, "Sockless Jerry," Populist congressman from Kansas, endorsed Donnelly for the presidency and a boomlet developed, Donnelly set aside such ambitions, preferring instead, he said, the gubernatorial nomination in Minnesota.

When the People's party convention opened in Omaha on July 2, 1892, Donnelly was the keynote speaker. His emphasis was upon the role of the party in an America in crisis. He concluded:

This battle in which we are employed is the battle of mankind. This continent is the last great camping ground of the human race. If liberty fails here, it fails forever. Every oppressed nation in the world is looking upon this convention to discover whether the . . . stars and stripes shall float across the country steadily rising generation after generation to higher levels of culture and civilization, or if it shall float a solemn mockery above a land cursed as Europe is cursed—the middle class driven off the land, while concentrated in the hands of a few is the wealth provided by the toiler. . . .[9]

Returning to Minnesota, Donnelly was nominated by acclamation for the governorship by the party he had created. As he campaigned furiously, as he always did, he envisioned the world that his party and platform aspired to create. At first he transcribed his vision in brief notes to be used in speeches, but suddenly those notes assumed a life of their own and took the form of another novel.

III   The Golden Bottle

In the midst of his campaign for governor—he apologizes in his preface for the fact that "it is without that polish and elaboration which should always distinguish literary work. It was written hurriedly, much of it on my knee, in railroad cars, and at country hotels, in the intervals between campaign speeches"[10]—Donnelly wrote his third and last novel, *The Golden Bottle*. The novel, he also commented,

is the outgrowth of the great political struggle now going on, in this year of grace, 1892, in the United States; and it is intended to explain and defend, in the thin guise of a story, some of the new ideas put forth by the People's Party; and which concern, I sincerely believe, all the peoples of the civilized world. I have a hope that the interest of "the Golden Bottle" may not end with the events that gave it birth. (p. 3)

Unlike *Caesar's Column* and *Doctor Huguet*, *The Golden Bottle* avoids shocking situations, incidents, or subject matter, and is more clearly related to Stephen Crane's *Maggie: A Girl of the Streets* than it is to either of its predecessors among Donnelly's works. At the same time, it exudes from the beginning an air of optimism impossible to detect in either of the others—perhaps the result of the excitement engendered by the ferment of the campaign trail, where no candidate or platform is less than a winner to its partisans.

The story is that of a poor Kansas farm boy, Ephraim Benezet, whose lot is that of his time and class:

> It is the old, old story. Grasshoppers, poor crops, "pools," "trusts," "rings;" high prices for what we bought, low prices for what we sold; "burning the candle at both ends;" increasing taxation to support a lot of office-holding non-producers; an increasing family, with another lot of non-producers to support, much beloved, however, of their progenitors; debt, pinching economy, and, at last, that conditional sale of the homestead, which is disguised under the title of a "mortgage." More debt to pay interest on, more pinching, more grasshoppers, more pools, more "combines," and the end— foreclosure—wiping out—starting adrift, etc. (p. 9)

This early part of the novel is drawn in sharp detail, a realistic portrayal of the problems that had engendered Donnelly's radicalism and the rise of populism. In scenes reminiscent of Hamlin Garland's "Under the Lion's Paw," Donnelly describes the impact of the foreclosure that was every Western farmer's fate:

> No one spoke that night at supper. Mother was crying softly. Father looked the curses he did not speak. I sat at the foot of the table, furious at my own helplessness. The meagre meal was dispatched quickly. Our thoughts turned to the future. The future! It was like looking into the mouth of Hell. Oh, how many bitter hearts are there in this world! (p. 13)

The only possibility for a young countryman in such a predicament is to join the influx of farm boys to the city, the movement that also provides the substance of much of the early twentieth-century fiction and verse from writers as diverse as Theodore Dreiser, Floyd Dell, and Sherwood Anderson, Carl Sandburg, and Vachel Lindsay. The movement as a whole was perhaps engendered by stimuli as diverse as the young people who joined it, and certainly as much by ambition and curiosity as by economic displacement. But to Donnelly there was only one cause:

> I went out and talked to the stars as usual. But it was in vain. Useless was it to look to that quarter for help. I would go and hire out in the great city. But

what could I do? The great city! The great maw that swallows up the wretchedness of the country and makes it greater. . . . (p. 31)

But at this point Donnelly departs from the grimness of reality. The rest of the novel is a fantasy that provides the substance for a remarkably complete indictment of the political and economic structures of the world, a clearly defined panacea that will cure the illnesses of that structure, and an appealing fictional device that makes Aladdin's lamp the substance of adolescent dreams. At the same time, the fantasy, growing constantly more incredible as the story progresses, is firmly rooted in a great deal of realistic detail. Even so, it comes perilously close to absurdity just before the novel comes to its end.

The central image in the book is the Golden Bottle, "a curious-looking embossed gold flask or bottle," which is given Ephraim in the middle of the night by a mysterious, gentle-looking old man who introduces himself as "The Pity of God." The old man shows him the secret of the bottle: a single drop of the liquid it contains can turn iron nail into gold. Then he disappears as quickly as he had come, leaving Ephraim in the possession of the bottle.

Ephraim awakens in the morning to two competing realities: on one hand, the foreclosure of his father's mortgage and the ruin of his sweetheart, Sophie, whose family had already been evicted; and, on the other, the golden nail in his hand and the bottle at the foot of his bed. From this point the fantasy of the bottle becomes the reality of the story, as Ephraim learns to produce another golden nail. He then introduces the secret to his honest, skeptical parents and the gold into the community, implying at the time that he has discovered an ancient mound-builder's horde, a hint that leads to a massive assault on the now-secure farm by townspeople with shovels.

From this point on, Ephraim, with an unlimited supply of the gold that had been so scarce earlier, determines that he will right the economic wrongs of his age, first in his home county, by buying up mortgages and lending money at a low rate to farmers, then in the nation, as he becomes President of the United States, and finally in the world, as he leads a triumphant, heralded American army to liberate the masses of Europe from the economic forces that have enslaved them. In so doing he has, in effect, put into practice the basic principle of populism: the advocacy of a cheap, plentiful money. And he demonstrates its validity: not only does gold not become less valuable with its plentiful supply, but it continues to be the world's most valuable commodity for another reason—its ability to eliminate any evil just by its availability.

Although the possession of unlimited wealth inevitably makes Ephraim the most powerful man in the world, the path is not easy, as Ephraim allows his good nature to resist the temptations of power. First there is the moment of realization:

It is a delightful thing to feel rich. The difference between the mind of a wealthy man and that of a poor man is the difference between a room brilliantly lighted and one shrouded in darkness. In the first case every artistic form is revealed in the flood of illumination; in the other you bump your head against the walls and break your shins over the furniture; you grope, you crawl, you stumble, you swear. (p. 29)

From this initial reaction Ephraim makes predictable decisions, until he realizes that his luck has made him a public person, a curiosity, and a popular hero:

And here a curious transition was gradually worked within me. My only thought, when I realized that I held, in the golden bottle, the source of immense wealth, was that I would lift my family and myself out of wretchedness. I had visions of comfort, joy, the luxuries of life, books, music, pleasant society, travel, culture, everything that goes to delight the heart of man. But when I looked out over those swarming multitudes with their hot eyes and eager, drawn faces, and read in them the same old story of unending struggle with untoward circumstances, my heart went out to them, and I resolved to do all in my power to help them and make mankind nobler and happier. And something of this must have burned in my words and shone in my face, for the cheers were vociferous. And so from town to town our progress was a continuous ovation. (p. 37)

Not only are Ephraim's self-perception and that of the crowd changing, but so is that of the editor of the newspaper that has served as the voice of the exploiters, under the name *The Voice of Freedom*. In the first account of Ephraim's gold, the editor's account describes him as

Ephe Benezet . . . a long-legged, ignorant, gawky fellow, too lazy to work to help his father out of debt, but given (so the neighbors say) to lying around and reading trashy books. It is supposed that his story is true and that he ploughed these nails up, and that they are the relics of some by-gone age. . . . (pp. 38–39)

But as the editor realizes that the event was not merely an isolated incident, his perception changes:

The same young man, Mr. Ephraim Benezet, son of that worthy gentleman,

Mr. John Benezet, who lives five miles from town, has returned and sold Mr. Burke twenty-one more golden nails. . . . The young gentleman, Mr. Ephraim Benezet, who has on both occasions brought in the golden objects to sell, is a young man of fine intelligence and a great student—a credit, indeed, to Butler County. (p. 39)

As more gold is produced and sold, the public image of the Benezets changes even more drastically. In the next issue Ephraim finds

the whole first page filled with a glowing article about ourselves and the gold mine. Nothing that ingenuity or industry could scrape together to satisfy the insatiable curiosity of the public. . . . There was a full account of the ancient Aztec civilization . . . portraits of our whole family; the one of myself being especially handsome and conspicuous . . . an account of our pedigree, dating back to the Mayflower . . . a glowing biography of my mother's great-granduncle, who was a sutler's clerk in the Revolutionary War . . . a picture of our tumble-down house, touched up to look like quite a handsome mansion . . . our poor old fly-bitten bull represented as rampaging down a forty-acre field. . . . The touch of gold had beautified our faces, our dwelling, our characters, our pedigree, our stock, and even our poultry. . . . (pp. 40–41)

Ephraim perceives within his own family inroads of inevitable corruption as his father begins to speak of "the common people," but he nonetheless begins his work. First he lends money in the county at two percent interest to pay off mortgages held at exorbitant rates; he gathers a group around him to carry on his mission, paying them enough so that they can be trusted; he rescues Sophie from a jail cell in the city, where she had been imprisoned after protecting her honor with force, and he marries her; he begins to produce gold on a massive scale and, his old story no longer adequate, he reveals that he has discovered the elixir long sought by alchemists; in time, he dines with the president, and he is invited to address Congress upon the welfare of the people, a speech that echoes those being given by Donnelly on political stumps across Minnesota at the time. Using his own success in eliminating poverty from his own Kansas county through cheap money as an example, Ephraim reiterates the principles of populism perceived and preached by Donnelly for so long:

Let us get clear of all this nonsense. Let us relegate the worship of gold and silver to the region of witchcraft and spooks, and all the other trash of the under-fed undeveloped past. Let us establish several propositions:
1. That real money is not a commodity, but a governmental measure of values, to facilitate the exchange of commodities.

2. That the government must furnish its people with an adequate supply of this medium of exchange, just as it is in duty bound to furnish them with an adequate supply of postage stamps.

3. That this medium shall bear the government stamp and be full legal-tender for all debts public and private; otherwise it is not money, but disqualified rubbish.

4. That it should be made of the cheapest and lightest material, with a reasonable degree of durability; and these qualities we find in paper.

5. That it should be so abundant as to enable the community to do business on a cash basis, and not pay interest on the bulk of its transactions. (p. 130)

In spite of the ovation with which his speech is received, its ultimate implementation is defeated by forces that Ephraim learns are those of plutocracy: the idea is impossible, the press proclaims; no nation can support such a system without collapse; government notes will fall; business will become bankrupt; democracy will disappear.

As in *Caesar's Column*, Donnelly digresses to a long debate between the plutocratic voice, heard through the newspapers, and Ephraim, the voice of the masses in their demand for cheap money. Ultimately, Sophie, who has organized a Women's Aid Society, detects the effects of the plutocracy's propaganda among her people: they are beginning to believe the propaganda and see Ephraim as a danger who must be destroyed.

Faced with this threat, Ephraim organizes his support into a Brotherhood, but, unlike that in *Caesar's Column*, this is the Brotherhood of Justice, dedicated to reform through the political system. It works, and Ephraim first builds a perfectly planned town to show what might be done, and then enters politics as the presidential nominee of the People's party. In spite of attempts at assassination, he is swept into office. Plutocracy is paralyzed, and in his inaugural address Ephraim makes clear his plan to liberate not only America but the world:

The new civilization must extend a helping hand to the old. The whole moral influence of this giant republic must be thrown upon the side of the people in their struggles with kingcraft. . . . We must withdraw our ministers from every kingdom and empire in Europe, to emphasize our detestation of systems of government which makes paupers of the producers of all wealth, and drive those paupers across the Atlantic to break down our own prosperity. . . . (p. 203)

This populist version of Manifest Destiny terrorizes European as well as American plutocracy; Europe mobilizes; two million Americans fight for the privilege of enlisting; Canada is quickly occupied by the Brotherhood, to the cheers of its people; the provinces become American territories, and Canadians rush to enlist for the campaigns in Europe. "One touch of liberty made the whole world kin" (p. 209), Donnelly muses. What appears to be the beginning of a major war becomes instead a repetition of the Canadian experience, as Ephraim's troops, led by "General Sophie" as well as himself, land first in Ireland, then in England, and finally on the continent. Ephraim's comment as England becomes his by acclamation describes the entire campaign: "England was not conquered. She had liberated herself. The grand, self-governing race had leaped at one bound to the full stature of freedom" (p. 222).

Ireland has fallen in one day, England in another, and Germany in a three-day campaign. Nothing remains but to sweep up the remainder as rapidly, and establish the new order. In the final cataclysm in Russia, the economic and social Armageddon, General Sophie cries with delightful naiveté to Ephraim, "'Didn't we give it to em! Oh, if Kansas could have seen it!'" (p. 262). But Ephraim and Donnelly reflect that "the thousand years of peace and happiness and love had begun, amid the corpses of that bloody battlefield; the last battlefield of the ages" (p. 263).

Ephraim's triumphal conquest of Europe, as much a victory for America as for himself, his gold bottle, or his economics, antedates that of Woodrow Wilson by a quarter-century, but the two visits are curiously alike, as man and country become fused in the popular mind into a promise for a new, peaceful, and humane future. Like Wilson, Ephraim has a plan, and again the two are curiously alike. Wilson had his Fourteen Points and his League of Nations, and Ephraim his new Christianity, placing Christ above creed, and his "Universal Republic." But whereas Wilson's plan a generation later was to be wrecked on the shoals of nationalism, American as well as European, Ephraim's triumph is complete, as his Christianity and his government are firmly established. The headquarters of the new Universal Republic are to be at a site for Donnelly symbolically appropriate:

There were the Azore Islands. They had been the mountain peaks of the drowned "Atlantis," whose history was told by the Greek priests to Solon, and recorded for posterity by Plato; the great world that lies in the background of human history; the mighty empire said to have been drowned by God for its sins. (pp. 274–75)

With the republic established under a system of government not unlike that proclaimed by the refugees from the cataclysm in *Caesar's Column*, Ephraim sees not permanence but the beginning of a new cycle in human history, one which is part of a much greater cosmic cycle like that described in *Atlantis* and *Ragnarok*:

> It seemed to me that, with such a system, peace, order, and the highest civilization would endure on earth until some cosmical catastrophe wiped the human family off the planet, in another "Ragnarok." (p. 277)

This Utopia, secure under a world government more nearly like the League of Nations proposed by Wilson fifteen years after Donnelly's death than like any other republic the world had ever known, is governed by principles reminiscent of the Fourteen Points upon which Wilson would seek to bring peace to the world:

> "The Universal Republic" should protect each nation in its established rights, boundaries, etc.; it should secure to each a republican form of government; it should aid in the suppression of internal rebellions; it should maintain a small army and navy, with power to call upon its constituent powers for further naval or military forces when necessary. It should have the further right to communicate with the congresses of each nation, and offer, from time to time, such advice as it saw fit, upon matters essential to the welfare of the people; but with no power to otherwise interfere in the domestic affairs of a country, except where a nation refused to submit to its decrees, under appeal, in contests with another republic. (p. 276)

With his populist Utopia established, Donnelly might have ended the novel, just as he might have ended it at any of several possible places earlier; but he had two important details to complete. First, it remained for him to bring Sophie and Ephraim home to America and to Kansas, through adulation greater than they had received in Europe and far greater than Wilson was to receive when he carried his plan to the people in 1919. At last, worn out by the journey, they reach Chicago, "that marvelous city . . . the eighth wonder of the world, with a man's age and the wealth and power of an empire" (p. 293), and, after a great reception, they retire for a night's rest. Then Donnelly concludes with the second detail.

When Ephraim awakens in the morning Sophie is not by his side, and he is not in the Palmer House but in the garret of his old farm home. Only reluctantly, with a great deal of torment, can he accept the reality: it has all been but a dream. Even worse are the facts: the farm is about to be foreclosed and it is reported that Sophie, in remorse over her life of shame, has hanged herself in Kansas City. At this, "I whirled around as if I had been struck on the head with an axe, and fell prostrate on the floor" (p. 297).

But again, at this moment of hopelessness, Donnelly is unwilling to end the novel, and, once more returned to sanity, Ephraim prays in his garret: "'. . . O Father Supreme, if Thou didst not make this world as a cruel jest, have mercy upon it. . . . Do not make us and forget us, O Lord God'" (pp. 300–301).

At that moment reality vanishes again and fantasy returns in the form of "an elderly gentleman, arrayed in the costume of the seventeenth century,—knee-britches, cocked hat, gold buckles on shoes, sword by side, ruffled shirt, projecting, stiff collar and all—" (p. 302), who introduces a creative, fantastic idea that Donnelly might have turned into another *Atlantis* or *Ragnarok*:

"... I am a pictorial reproduction, on the retina of a human intellect, of something that lived and breathed and loved and sinned and died two hundred years ago in bonny, brisk England. . . . O Nature! Nature!" . . . "Nature is full of marvels; two hundred years ago this toggery, which I am parading in, impressed itself on my vital principle, and now my vital principle is able to impress it on yours; a photograph of a photograph; and a thousand years from now you may convey it, perchance, to some fellow in Mars. . . ." (pp. 303–304)

But the appearance of the energetic old gentleman is as functional as that of "The Wrath of God"; not only does he introduce Ephraim to another consciousness in another sphere, but he lectures kindly on the nature of life—"the angels have made nothing more wonderful than some of the inventions of man" (p. 312); he denies the rumor about Sophie—"That tin-peddler was a liar" (p. 305); he tells the truth about Ephraim's health—"... You've got no consumption" (p. 307); and most importantly, he gives Ephraim sound advice—"go to work. . . . Write out your dream" (p. 307). Refusing, however, to answer Ephraim's last question—"...What is to be the final outcome of man's civilization on earth? Will it end in a cataclysm?" (p. 312)—he vanishes into nothingness, leaving Ephraim eager to get on with the job ahead.

The visitor's refusal to answer and the eagerness with which Ephraim faces a future devoid of fantasy but rewarding in work and in goals introduces a note of optimism at the end of the book that is new to Donnelly's fiction. Donnelly does not deny the final cataclysm in this novel, nor does he suggest that man can circumvent whatever may be the ultimate cyclical fate of civilization as we know it; but he does suggest, with emphasis untempered by a note of penitence like that with which he ended *Doctor Huguet*, that man can improve his lot by intelligent planning and constant appeals to the innate wisdom of the majority.

Like *Caesar's Column* and *Doctor Huguet*, *The Golden Bottle* stems from three sources: from Donnelly's interest in the gothic substance of the fantasy, from his economic and political conviction, and from his perception of social ills. Donnelly's fantasy takes recurring forms, in each novel centering on a particular symbolic representation or reversion; thus the time lapse and the monument to horror in *Caesar's Column* are paralleled in *Dr. Huguet* by the transformation of human characteristics resulting in another variety of horror. But in *The Golden Bottle* the central symbol is not horrible at all; rather, it is an obvious, barbed parody of man's nonsensical preoccupation with the acquisition of something as intrinsically worthless as gold.

The central symbol is directly related to Donnelly's conviction that money has no value other than that which is intrinsic to its function as a medium of exchange. No Free Silver advocate, like so many of his Western associates, Donnelly was convinced that, given enough money readily available, the social evils of the age, those graphically described in the book—rural poverty, farm decline, sweatshops, dishonest journalism, crime—can be overcome, and in their place a society can be constructed that enjoys temperance, women's suffrage, nationalized railroads, home ownership, free education, and a perfect Jeffersonian society, not only in the countryside but in the cities as well.

Curious in the novel is the consistency with which Donnelly reflects his old prejudices—the selection of the Azores as the headquarters for the new nation, the shadow of cataclysm, the preoccupation with conflict as perhaps the only means by which social evils may eventually be overcome.

Like its two predecessors, *The Golden Bottle* is not a conventional novel, and it is pointless to apply conventional critical standards to it. Rather, like Donnelly's other attempts at fiction, it is at once a vivid presentation of a world devoid of kindness, mercy, and soft money, and a warning that, without redress, social cataclysm, whether mindless rebellion or iron become gold, is inevitable. Furthermore, Donnelly sees the novel form essentially as a vehicle for ideas and a medium whereby social change may be brought about.

Nevertheless, in spite of its excesses and structural flaws, its lapses into absurdity, and its triteness in concept and execution, *The Golden Bottle* has several strengths that make it more than a mere exercise in propaganda. It antedates later trends in the development of naturalistic fiction—not merely focusing on the exploitation of women but making them central characters; exploring the social illnesses of the city as well as the countryside; suggesting the existence of natural forces beyond our finite understanding; functioning not merely as political polemic but as careful social criticism. It attempts to explore a probability of motivation beyond that defined by Howells and James and approaching that of Crane and Dreiser.

Perhaps the most curious aspect of this novel, unlike its two predecessors, is its blend of the pessimism inherent in determinism—in Donnelly's case that of certain natural catastrophe—and the progressive optimism that was to become so evident in the politics of Progressivism and the New Freedom nearly a generation in the future.

There are two other curious foreshadowings in the book: first, just as Ephraim's symbolic campaign metaphorically describes Donnelly's literal crusades over the previous thirty years, it clearly parallels that of Woodrow Wilson that was yet to come. In its confident idealism, its unconscious arrogance, its moralistic righteousness, Ephraim's crusade, like Wilson's, becomes an extension of a mission accepted, if not demanded, nearly two hundred years before, a dedicated sense of purpose and duty that has recurred as cyclically as Donnelly's alleged cataclysms, throughout the history of North America, and a mission that, he predicts, will predictably recur as far into the future as we maintain our American identity.

The second parallel has been pointed out on a number of occasions: the blend of delightful and horrible fantasy in Donnelly's work that anticipates Frank Baum's *The Wonderful Wizard of Oz*, published in 1900. Less dogmatic, more delightful, and more durable than Donnelly's fantasy, Baum's work continues to please long after the causes of populism have become history, and its symbolism has become wonderfully literal in the process; but its populist origins are clear.

The Golden Bottle had been finished as the gubernatorial campaign ended, and Donnelly summed up his feelings in his diary on election eve:

I have conversed with 10,000 persons, wrote a novel, prepared two "broadsides" of eight pages each; carried on a large correspondence and supervised the whole campaign. I hope to win and yet nothing is certain. . . . I have had a grand campaign; tremendous meetings—great enthusiasm. I shall have done some good even if I am beaten.[11]

In the election, however, Donnelly was beaten badly, and he confided in his diary that he was "Beaten! Whipped! Smashed! . . ."

CHAPTER 6

Crusade's End

I The American People's Money

WITH the publication of *The Golden Bottle*, Donnelly's literary career was largely at an end, although in the years between his defeat for the governorship of Minnesota in 1892 and his defeat for the vice presidency of the United States in 1900 he delivered dozens of speeches, wrote numerous articles, and published two separate works, *The American People's Money* in 1895 and *The Cipher in the Plays and on the Tombstone* in 1899.

The American People's Money was written, according to Donnelly, at the request of the publisher; he commented wryly that "Even the philosophers have to bow to the humors of the many-headed monster—the public."[1] But the philosopher in the book—Hugh Sanders, a midwestern farmer who is clearly Donnelly's alter ego—creates public opinion rather than bowing to it. The tract takes the form of a discussion between Sanders and a Chicago banker, James Hutchinson, on a train going West. In the emphasis in their argument on the necessity for cheap, plentiful currency, Donnelly echoes the thesis advanced in *The Golden Bottle* that the only source of permanent, universal prosperity is money readily available to all. But in keeping with the spirit of the liberal political climate of the time, he does not insist upon a fiat currency, at least immediately; rather, as in other tracts of the times, most notably *Coin's Financial School* by W. H. Harvey and other similar economic works, Donnelly advocates that under the current metallic money system, silver should be as readily usable as gold.

Interestingly, Donnelly's persona here bears a resemblance to the image of Donnelly that emerges in *Donnelliana*, the campaign biography written by Everett W. Fish in 1892, the same Fish with whom Donnelly had enjoyed a long political love-hate relationship. In both portrayals, Donnelly is the articulate, wise, knowledgeable philosopher, and his conquest of the opposition by charm and reason as well as the sheer weight of evidence is inevitable.

104

Although Donnelly makes no apology for *The American People's Money* other than its value as an economic and political statement of position, in many ways it belongs in the array of his fiction, just as his novels must invariably be considered as tracts. The structure is based on a prolonged conversation that echoes the long explanatory dialogues so prominent in *Caesar's Column, Doctor Huguet,* and *The Golden Bottle.* There are also echoes of George Bernard Shaw, who in *Widower's Houses* (1892) and *Mrs. Warren's Profession* (1893) had begun to explore in drama in England the subject matter that Donnelly and his fellow Populists were exploring in fiction and pseudofiction in the United States.

Typical of the exchange is that between Hutchinson, the banker, and Sanders, the farmer, on the subject of the Darwinian principles that John D. Rockefeller, Sr., and Andrew Carnegie had adapted to the economic realm:

[Hutchinson] ". . . Competition must necessarily force down wages, according to the 'iron law of wages,' to the lowest point of compensation for which the laborer will be able to live, perform his work and raise another to take his place when his time has come. This rule runs through all nature. Darwin calls it the 'survival of the fittest. . . .'"

[Sanders] "Precisely, . . . and the man who will work for ten cents must eventually supplant the man who asks for a quarter."

"Exactly."

"And there is no limit to it?"

"None whatever. The operation of the law is inflexible and inexorable."

"Then it follows that as the great mass of mankind are toilers with muscles, the great mass of mankind must be reduced to the lowest possible condition compatible with continued existence?"

"Of course."

"So that the Chinaman who works for six cents a day and lives on a diet of rice, flavored with an occasional rat, is a type of what the American citizen of the producing class is to be in the near future?"

"It seems so; the law is inflexible."

"But does not Darwin admit that the human race, by reason of its intelligence, rises above the limitations of his great theory? . . .

"Thus, you perceive, that the doctrine of 'the survival of the fittest' does not stand when it comes in conflict with human intelligence. . . . Primitive man had not the size of his giant foes, nor their strength, nor their swiftness, but he had intellect, and to intellect all laws yield.

". . . And, if necessary, the free man will exterminate any new aristocracy which may rise up to reduce him to universal poverty (to six cents a day and rice and rats), just as he blotted out the fierce creatures of prehistoric times. . . ."[2]

Not only does Donnelly's simple farmer, like the Brother Jona-thans of American rural tradition, vanquish his foe by his superior innate intelligence and logic, but he has facts and figures at his command, as well as a gift for language. As the book closes, his graphic description of the lot of the poor reduces an interested young lady listener to tears. Donnelly, as Sanders, concludes eloquently:

> "That is night and its horror. This is day and its glories.
> Choose ye between them.
> The bell tolls the hour of destiny and doom."

The second publication of Donnelly's last decade was, like the first, a tract, but it did not have the political or economic support enjoyed by the earlier. Instead, it combines with earlier works, *Atlantis*, *Ragnarok*, and *The Great Cryptogram*, in particular, to give Donnelly the reputation of a mountebank or crank in some circles and a prophetic genius in others. This was *The Cipher in the Plays and on the Tombstone*, his second attempt to prove the hidden genius of Francis Bacon. The product of nearly eight years of work, it was written, as Donnelly comments in the Preface,

to patiently advance through the thistles and cockle-burrs, and help us settle the great, and enduring controversy, as to whether the immortal plays were written by the play-actor of Stratford, or the greatest intellect that ever appeared on this theatre of human action—the transcendent Francis Bacon.[3]

Unfortunately, however, Donnelly's critics and even some of his friends felt that he had gone too far, asserting that Bacon had not only written Shakespeare's works but those of Marlowe and Cervantes as well. The book did not sell, and, although Donnelly proposed a sequel, *Ben Jonson's Cipher*, to William Waldorf Astor, who had supported the earlier work, Astor refused to support it. *The Cipher in the Plays and on the Tombstone* was Donnelly's last book.

II *Last Writings*

Between early 1893, when Donnelly was once more rebuilding the liberal-radical political element in Minnesota in his own image, and his death in 1901, he combined his political and literary interests in editing and publishing the *Representative*, a weekly newspaper devoted to discussing those issues and positions that had divided liberal forces in Minnesota and led to their defeat.

In the *Representative* Donnelly advocated the remonetization of silver, a necessary compromise of his real desire for the old greenback demand for fiat money. Elected vice president of the American Bimetallic League in July 1893, Donnelly spoke at its conference in Chicago in August. There he impressed William Jennings Bryan by his demand for the unlimited coinage of silver.

That fall, as depression intensified, Donnelly continued his demand for loose money, and he demanded too that the government take the necessary steps to alleviate conditions. Stung by criticism from those who insisted that he would sacrifice American freedom, he demanded rhetorically in the *Representative*:

What is freedom worth to a man who is dying of hunger? Can you keep a room warm, next winter, with the thermometer at 30° below zero by reading the Declaration of Independence? Whenever the prosperity of a people is attacked, their liberty and morality are both assailed.[4]

Aware that the passage of time and the closing of the frontier had made ridiculous the traditional injunctions to seek one's fortune elsewhere, as he had done nearly forty years before, he commented that "there are no more Minnesotas on the planet; and every day the battle of life will grow fiercer." A few months later, he wrote:

We have practically reached the limit of our available free-land supply. That free-land has been the safety valve of Europe and America. When that valve is closed, swarming mankind every day will increase the danger of explosion. Nothing can save the world but the greatest wisdom, justice and fair play.[5]

Donnelly may indeed have read Frederick Jackson Turner's "Problems in American History" or news reports of "The Significance of the Frontier in American History," given earlier that year in Chicago; but he read implications into the end of geographic mobility that are more immediate and more dangerous than Turner had contemplated.

Donnelly's articles in the *Representative* provided much of the fuel for the modern assertions that Populism and Donnelly himself were anti-Semitic or protofascist. In the November 8, 1893, issue, in response to the attempt to repeal Chinese exclusion acts, Donnelly conjured the vision of the "Chinaman, who can live on rice and rats, work for 30 cents a day, put down by the elbow of every American mechanic, to reduce him to the same fare and wages";[6] the farmers he saw replaced with "rat-tailed slant-eyed Mongolians, where one wife will do for a whole township, and neither public schools nor churches will be needed."[7]

As his campaign against the gold standard intensified in 1894, Donnelly directed much of his argument and polemics against the Rothschilds, as did much of the Populist press, and with them he assaulted the mythical Jewish moneylenders of whom the Rothschilds had become the stereotypes. But, he insisted, he did not attempt to attack the Jews as a people or a religion:

A plutocratic Jew is no worse than a plutocratic Christian—in fact, he is half as bad. For the Jew, for nearly 2,000 years has been proscribed, persecuted, and hunted down; fenced into the corners of towns; hounded, pelted, and stoned by ignorant populations when the Jews were preserving the knowledge of the one true God in the midst of an idolatrous and degraded world. . . . Karl Marx, the Jewish reformer, faces Rothschild, the Jew plutocrat. . . . We are fighting Plutocracy not because it is Jewish or Christian, but because it is Plutocracy. . . . We would be sorry to be understood as saying one word that would pander to prejudice against any man because of his race, religion, nationality, or color.[8]

When the "APA," the American Protective Association, began its rapid growth during the depression of 1893, attracting native Protestant workers with its insistence that the depression was the result of a Catholic plot to flood America with Catholics and eventually conquer it for the Pope, Donnelly opposed it immediately. The APA, with ties to Republicanism largely because most Catholics were Democrats, represented to Donnelly a threat both to American principles and to liberal politics. He wrote that

the founder of the society, Henry F. Bowers, of Clinton, Iowa, is an attorney, in receipt of a salary from the Chicago and Northwestern Railroad Company; and he is reported to have said that when they got the society fairly well started "there would be no more strikes! . . ." The society was established to distract public opinion from the economic questions of the hour; and preventing all producers uniting against a common enemy, by setting them to fighting each other over questions of the next world; or old world memories of ages past.[9]

Although Donnelly supported the Cuban rebels editorially, advocating American aid to their cause, he was strongly antiimperialist. When the *Maine* was sunk in Havana harbor, Donnelly refused to believe that war was imminent, but when it came he advocated a graduated income tax, to prevent profit from the war and the loss of human life. "It would have been cheaper to have bought Cuba outright from Spain," he wrote. "It would have saved many millions of dollars and many thousands of human lives."[10] On August 17,

1898, he wrote, "New and serious questions open before us." On June 1, 1899, as the army began its pacification campaign in the Philippines, he wrote that "our government should not violate the laws of civilized warfare and indulge in an indiscriminate slaughter of men, women, and children."

During these years, using the editorial column of the *Representative* to express his views on virtually every issue on the national and international scene, Donnelly remained active in Minnesota and national Populist politics, with the paper as one of his most effective instruments. Although he had said that at the end of the 1893 legislative session he would no longer be a candidate for public office, proposing "to separate from all members of the senate on terms of kindness and good will," he remained in controversial conflict to the end of his life. In June 1893, at the Anti-Trust Conference in Chicago, he made a series of demands on the federal government—seizure of coal fields, nationalization of monopolies, elimination of legal protections for trusts, among others—but his proposals were defeated. He attacked the anthracite coal combine time after time and then turned to attack tax evasion by lumbermen in a campaign that shook lumber-producing Minnesota for months. He was indeed "the most popular man in Minnesota—between elections," as he delighted in telling crowds at rallies.

When Coxey's Army marched on Washington, Donnelly, perhaps recalling *Caesar's Column*, observed in the *Representative* that "we do not like the movement of 10,000 or 100,000 men, now organized under Mr. Coxey and advancing on Washington. A vast array of starving men becomes a terrible thing:—once started, no one can control them. . . ."[11]

In July 1894 he strongly supported the American Railway Union, commenting in its behalf that "the settlement of the slavery question inconvenienced a great many people."[12] Though he was the keynote speaker in the Populist Convention in Minneapolis in July, he was unable to keep the convention focused upon economic reform and away from the women's suffrage and liquor questions, both increasingly prominent among urban reformers. He was renominated for the state senate but lost in the Republican sweep in the fall. He commented, "The pine land investigations will cease; the state elevator will be heard no more; the reduction of interest on money will be dropped. Nothing will be done for the good of the people. And the people deserve it. And they will suffer for it."[13]

In 1895 Donnelly fought to unite the party again, attempting to remain neutral as the Bryan forces sought to capture it. Although he was spoken of briefly in early 1896 as a potential presidential candidate, he was more pleased with the terror the rumor brought to some Minnesota factions than he was with any such possibility. As Bryan neared and then captured the Democratic nomination with a platform essentially Populist, Donnelly withheld his public support. Even at the Populist convention in St. Louis, after a brief demonstration demanding Donnelly's nomination collapsed and the party accepted Bryan as its nominee, Donnelly remained aloof. Then, in early fall, charmed and flattered by Bryan, he fell into line and campaigned widely in Illinois, Kansas, and Missouri, as well as Minnesota. Bryan lost badly to McKinley, but Donnelly was elected to the legislature. He wrote, "We shall probably poke our head out of the cyclone cellar, and anxiously inquire if the storm has blown over. It is well that a few specimen Populists should survive, so that people may know what the breed looked like."[14] He filed his campaign expenses, as required by the new Minnesota Pure Election Law: "It amounts to the enormous sum of $3.98. . . ."

Though tired and without a substantial party following, Donnelly remained a controversial power in the legislature as well as in the party. In the national Populist convention of August 1898 he lost the presidential nomination by nine votes, but he was unanimously nominated for the vice presidency. Privately, with no hope of winning, he saw the nomination as a good advertisement for his books and lectures. He announced that he would not seek reelection to the legislature that fall but instead would concentrate on his national candidacy.

But as he began the campaign, his age and health began for the first time to betray him. On July 4, 1900, while speaking at a rally, he nearly collapsed, and he returned home to a diagnosis first of heat prostration and later of a mild stroke. On November 3, 1900, he wrote in his diary:

I am 69 today. I begin to feel very old, although I preserve my youthful appearance remarkably:—my hair is not yet gray; but my legs are weak. I drag my feet when I walk. My ill fortune pursues me. If I had not had a partial stroke of palsey, I would have made the whole U.S. ring with my appeals for the Mid-Road ticket.[15]

The outcome of the election was predictable; equally predictable, as Donnelly knew, was the fact that it would be his last, as indeed it was. Two months later, just after midnight on January 1, 1901, as the nineteenth century died and with it the cause of Populist reform, Donnelly suffered another attack. He died quietly in bed, and four decades of political and intellectual warfare came to an end.

CHAPTER 7

Retrospect

I *Donnelly's Achievement*

THE significance of the coincidental date of Donnelly's death on the morning of the first day of the twentieth century seemed to portend to some of his obituarists that he would remain, at best, a footnote in the history of nineteenth-century American radicalism. For much of the twentieth century, intellectual historians seemed to agree. Although in his lifetime descriptions of him ranged from the visionary, as his supporters saw him, to the radical, crank, or crackpot of his opponents, it was evident as Populism merged with the American political mainstream that his proposed reforms were, in retrospect, relatively innocuous.

Nevertheless, in spite of his relative lack of personal success, particularly in partisan political warfare, it became evident by the mid-twentieth century that he was not a typical unsuccessful politician. In spite of his failures, Donnelly's career and his writings could not only shed a great deal of light upon the political and intellectual history of his time, but could also, because of his strong influence on public developments, give a good deal of insight into the nature of the political process as it responded to his energy and ideas. This discovery led to the first major study of Donnelly as a political figure, that of Martin Ridge, published in 1962.

The rediscovery of Donnelly the remarkably well-documented political philosopher and activist led to another rediscovery: that of Donnelly the natural philosopher, the antiutopian novelist, and the cryptographer, or in other words, of Donnelly the writer. Donnelly's writings had long been known; indeed, both *Atlantis* and *Caesar's Column* could be considered best-sellers, and his work had remained the subject of study and influence by a variety of cultists for a variety of reasons. It finally became not only possible but desirable that he be studied as a writer as well as a politician, political theorist, and reformer.

Donnelly's career as a writer parallels his career as a political figure in several ways. Both were unconventional; both involved similar historical theories, whether natural or political; and both reflected his concern with reform. Often, in addition, the writings were essentially extensions of his political career, based upon the same ideas that fired his political crusades, and the ideological bases for the works made them as unique in their way as his political career was in its way. In each case there is a logical progression more evident now than in the past.

Donnelly was not a great writer, nor did he pretend to be; he was not a great original thinker, although there is evidence to suggest that, on some occasions, at least, he was convinced that he was; and the perspective of our time recognizes that his role in political history, perhaps because of his disregard for convention, will be much greater than his place in literary history, again for the very same reason.

Nevertheless, Donnelly's literary career provides a good deal of insight into a particular phase of American literary history in a way that no other similar career of his age can. At the same time it offers much insight into the intellectual convictions that influenced and were, in turn, influenced by his political career. As in his political career, his literary career as a whole is far more significant than any of its parts.

In his writing as well as his political activism, Donnelly reflected his legal background and his love of language. A piece of writing—a novel, a tract, a scientific treatise, or a political essay—was to Donnelly an argument, to be like a legal brief, presented as logically, rationally, and eloquently as possible. It should have a purpose, a pragmatic point; and the task of the writer was to persuade his readers to accept it.

Thus, although Donnelly wrote easily and well, he never regarded his role as writer lightly, and he determined that each work should be as complete in detail as it was as an effective whole. Each work, too, it is evident, bears a logical relationship to each of the others, as well as to the context of the period of Donnelly's life in which it was written.

All the works, like his political career, are governed by similar concepts: regression rather than progression in change, whether evolutionary or cataclysmic; the potential for rational direction of change; the greater potential for tragedy in the ordinary human control of affairs. Each work, too, is a curious blend of faith in a past perfection and fear of coming disaster.

Donnelly's two pseudoscientific works, those with which he began his writing career, *Atlantis* and *Ragnarok*, are based on what are essentially mutually reinforcing concepts, that of the cataclysm and that of the cyclical structure of natural as well as social change. Each,

Donnelly was convinced, was a significant contribution to the literature of science, but, although the former sold well, neither of them received a serious scientific reception. Still, both are important, and not merely as scientific curiosities or support for pseudoscientific cultists. Both shed important light on Donnelly's political and social theories, particularly as they relate to his radical politics. Both works insist that physical, natural, and historical evidence suggests the existence of a society in the past that had attained near-perfection. This, as Donnelly insisted, was Plato's Atlantis—the prototype of the Garden of Eden. When the people of Atlantis fell from virtue, natural catastrophe, perhaps unleashed by a vengeful God, destroyed them, thus providing man with the substance of his myths, his religions, and his folklore.

This beginning is essentially the vision of the past provided by the agrarian myth or myth of the garden, which Donnelly merges with the Atlantean myth of classical Greece. For the story of the cataclysm that destroyed it, he turns to Ragnarok, the god of Norse mythology who destroys the sinful world that it may regenerate itself and rediscover its virtue.

This relationship between the natural order and moral behavior, a nearly complete rejection of scientific views of a neutral universe governed by predictable natural laws in favor of the roles of morality and justice, is reflected in Donnelly's novels, *Caesar's Column*, *Doctor Huguet*, and *The Golden Bottle*. In each, Donnelly examines, in microcosm, the situation that brings about cataclysmic destruction. In the first, economic oppression brings about the revolt of the masses and a mindless assault that threatens the destruction of society; in the second, racial injustice brings about a tragic reversal of roles; and in the third, economic reform purportedly brings about a new order through war.

Interestingly, although with the single exception of his support for the Civil War Donnelly never advocated any reform other than that to be brought about through the ballot box—an evolutionary rather than revolutionary process—in each of the novels he insists that the lot of the oppressed classes has passed beyond the point where evolutionary solutions are possible, and in each he sees too the fact that a full solution is possible. In *Caesar's Column* the revolution degenerates to the point where salvation is impossible, and the few just people must flee to a primitive, remote Eden; in *Doctor Huguet*, only one conversion results from a willful suspension of natural law; and *The Golden Bottle* resolves its plot—and abandons protest— with the use of a dream that temporarily suspends reality.

Nevertheless, the political and social implications of the novels are

clear: man has not yet exhausted the potential for reform—
significantly *Caesar's Column* is set a century in the future, and the
situation is not quite so grim in the others—but it is at his peril and the
peril of society as a whole that he continues to delay that reform. If he
refuses his opportunity to use the ballot box wisely, mindless wrath,
whether of an outraged people or a wrathful god, will provide the
punishment that has been so richly earned.

II *Donnelly's Significance*

Donnelly wrote a great deal more than these five books: letters,
speeches, editorials, pamphlets, verse, and items that defy classifi-
cation; but is upon these five works that any assessment of his place in
literary history must be based. The flaws inherent in them—
didacticism, polemics, structural and stylistic flaws, possible traces of
incipient fascism and racism—make it impossible to rank Donnelly
high among his contemporary writers, and his obvious literary
shortcomings, together with his equally obvious political shortcomings, prevent any consideration of him as other than an interesting,
well documented, and often fascinating figure on the political stage of
the late nineteenth century.

Yet to dismiss Donnelly so casually on the basis of either aspect of
his career or both would be unjust. In microcosm, in his careers as
politician, promoter, and writer, Donnelly, more than any other
figure of his time, personifies the intellectual foundation of the
reform impulse in his time as it sought a political base and an
articulate, persuasive voice, a voice often Donnelly's own.

Donnelly's careers, like the course of political and economic
reform in post-Civil War America, were compounded of idealism
and practicality, of rationality and a curious irrationality, of faith in
man and the future and a sense of impending doom, of a strong
humanitarian impulse and a fascination with violence, of faith in
evolutionary change and a preoccupation with revolution, of faith in
language and ideas as the means by which change may be brought
about and a concomitant intellectual snobbishness, of faith in the
common man and impatience with his slowness.

Donnelly's writings contain much of the ambiguity and incon-
sistency that combined to produce the reform impulse and the radical
movement in the last half of the nineteenth century. But equally
evident in both the period and Donnelly's work and his career are
consistencies that absorb the inconsistencies and make them essentially inconsequential. Perhaps the most consistent of the elements

that united and directed the radical impulse during those years were their underlying idealism and humanitarianism, their faith in justice and equality, their conviction that somehow, some way, man will one day construct a society in which virtue will triumph and evil receive its just punishment, a world in which the ideals of the past—of eighteenth-century rationalism and nineteenth-century romanticism—will merge in a new, perfect society in this world.

At the heart of Donnelly's work and the reform movement is a curious romanticism that looked always to the past for its ideal image of the future that it sought to bring into being. The search for the perfect, humane society in the late nineteenth century is an extension of that same search as it was characterized in the eighteenth century: a firm belief in natural rights, in progress and perfectibility, a conviction that somewhere in the universe rationality and law reign, that when all else fails man has the right to become a law unto himself and to destroy his oppressors that he may be free.

But just as Donnelly and his contemporaries were the products of the rational optimism of the eighteenth century, they were also products of the romantic tragedy of the nineteenth, a century that saw within reach the rebirth and affirmation of human freedom, dignity, and equality, all then withheld by the bloodiest war in history and snatched away, apparently irretrievably, by the forces against which the reformers struggled: the impersonal greed of a new industrialism; the political arrangements of a political system ostensibly based upon two competing parties that were for all practical purposes one; and the racist image of Jim Crow that had come to dominate much of the country, North as well as South.

The common national tragedy of the nineteenth century had its specific implications for the era's reformers and its personal implications for Donnelly. Just as the national tragedy of the nineteenth century was inherent in the blood-purge that Abraham Lincoln described in his second inaugural address as he defined the essence of the Civil War, it was inherent too in the human failure that followed it. To Lincoln the war had its origins and found its meaning in the divine impulse for justice that rules all things:

If God wills that it [the War] continue, until all the wealth piled by the bondman's two hundred and fifty years of unrequited toil shall be sunk, and until every drop of blood drawn with the lash, shall be paid by another drawn with the sword, as it was said three thousand years ago, so still it must be said "the judgements of the Lord, are true and righteous altogether."

With the purging completed, Lincoln foresaw a new nation with, as he remarked at Gettysburg a year and a half earlier, "a new birth of freedom," a nation in which the ideals of its origin in the eighteenth century would become real in the nineteenth, a nation that Donnelly and his contemporary reformers believed would become real. But neither Lincoln nor Donnelly foresaw the results of the war, as new forces were unleashed that enslaved men as firmly and hopelessly as those that had brought chattel slavery into being thousands of years earlier, marring the ideals of the new nation that grew out of the eighteenth-century search for human freedom.

The new national tragedy had its inception not only in Lincoln's death, perhaps foreshadowing the failure of human vision and the national will that followed it, but was brought into being by the new economic, political, and industrial forces made dominant by the war. Those postwar reformers—Ignatius Donnelly, Robert Ingersoll, John Peter Altgeld, and dozens of others—whose faith in the cause of human freedom burned brightly during the war, saw it threatened and nearly extinguished many times by the winds of change and circumstance in the thirty-five years that followed. But after each threat the flame burned more brightly, and each of them continued the struggle even as it seemed more hopeless.

For Altgeld, for Ingersoll, for Donnelly, and for most of the others, the personal record was a record of frustration and ultimate failure, a failure inherent in personal tragedy and having within it the seeds of incipient fascism, confusion, and prejudice that marred the reform movements that they led with such dedication. Each, in turn, passed into an obscurity compounded by the historical prominence accorded to the exploiters whom they opposed throughout their lives.

Even so, each of them marched with confidence through failure into an undeserved historical obscurity, a final vindicating battle and victory eluding them in their lifetimes. When Donnelly died at the beginning of the new century, the reform impulse had begun to enter the political mainstream, but the specific reforms that he sought were beyond the political horizon, where some of them remain even yet. Until they become reality, Donnelly's ultimate vindication eludes him.

Yet in the final sense Donnelly's life, his political ideals, and his works, a combination of reality, fantasy, and faith, are his own vindication and the ultimate victory that transcends the tragedy of his age. Throughout his life, even through failure and tragedy, he marched with confidence, his pace steady through the apparent vagaries and inconsistencies that marked it, his eyes focused upon the ultimate goals of personal and national fulfillment that he sought, in his ears the echo of the other battles that marked the sometimes faltering course of human freedom toward the ultimate victory that he was confident would come. In his view of nature and life as a cyclical flow between victory and defeat, he knew that the ultimate vision was never extinguished, but passed on in one form or another from one generation to another, and in his life and works he preserved and disseminated that vision during a period that saw it the target of the most powerful assault in our history. In each of his works, in the face of cataclysms, whether man-made or natural, he preserved that vision. Inherent in that preservation is his ultimate vindication as well as the meaning and significance of his life and works. Perhaps Donnelly will remain no more than a footnote in the political and literary history of a complex, dangerous era, but his omission impoverishes the history of a people as it still seeks to make an elusive ideal a human and political reality.

Donnelly's vivid imagination, his highly improbable or inaccurate science, his intellectual or personal shortcomings, may combine to make him look ridiculous, as some critics continue to insist that he was, but such an attempt is incomplete and short-sighted. Even at their weakest, his ideas and the motives that brought them into existence are, in the final sense, an extended metaphor of American life in his time and ours. More than three quarters of a century after his death that metaphor continues to unfold, and Donnelly's life, his career, and his works remain important keys to its meaning.

Notes and References

Chapter One

1. Biographical information and many documentary quotations, unless otherwise cited, come from Martin Ridge, *Ignatius Donnelly: Portrait of a Politician* (Chicago, 1962), the definitive political biography. I am responsible for interpretation of those facts and documents.

2. Quoted in Ridge, p. 5. In all quotations from the microfilm of the Donnelly papers I have verified my reading with that of Ridge.

3. Donnelly's lesson book, in the Donnelly Mss., Minnesota Historical Society; quoted in Ridge, p. 6.

4. Ignatius Donnelly, *The Mourner's Vision* (Philadelphia, 1850), pp. 1–2.

5. Quoted by John T. Flanagan in "A Letter from Holmes to Donnelly," *American Literature* 13 (March 1941), 60–61.

6. Reprinted in Alexander N. DeMenil, *The Literature of the Louisiana Territory* (St. Louis, 1904), pp. 179–81.

7. December 30, 1852; quoted in Ridge, pp. 9–10.

8. Quoted in Ridge, p. 10.

Chapter Two

1. Quoted in Ridge, p. 22.

2. Ibid., pp. 32–33.

3. Ibid., pp. 38–39.

4. Ibid., p. 67.

5. Ibid., p. 78.

6. Ibid., p. 80.

7. *St. Paul Dispatch*, Feb. 14, 1870; both quotations in Ridge, p. 129.

8. See Ridge, pp. 133–48, for a discussion of Donnelly's political evolution at this time.

9. From the Donnelly Mss., Minnesota Historical Society; quoted in Ridge, p. 140.

10. Quoted in Ridge, p. 195.

Chapter Three

1. Ignatius Donnelly, *Atlantis: The Antediluvian World* (New York, 1882), pp. 1–2. Further page references to this work are provided in the text.

2. From the Donnelly Mss., Minnesota Historical Society; quoted in Ridge, p. 202.

3. Quoted in Ridge, p. 204.

4. Ignatius Donnelly, *Ragnarok: The Age of Fire and Gravel* (New York, 1883), p. 2. Further page references to this work are provided in the text.

Chapter Four

1. Ignatius Donnelly, *The Great Cryptogram* (Chicago, 1887), pp. 13–14. Further page references to this work are provided in the text.

2. David Kahn, *The Codebreakers* (New York, 1967), p. 873.

3. Ibid., pp. 875–78.

4. February 12, 1888; quoted in Ridge, p. 234.

5. Quoted in Kahn, p. 877.

6. Quoted in Ridge, p. 238.

7. Ibid., pp. 240–41.

8. Ibid.

9. Ibid., p. 244.

10. Ignatius Donnelly, *Caesar's Column* (Chicago, 1890), p. 7. Further page references to this work are provided in the text.

Chapter Five

1. Quoted in Ridge, p. 283.

2. Ignatius Donnelly, *Doctor Huguet* (Chicago, 1891), p. 7. Further page references to this work are provided in the text.

3. Abraham Lincoln, in Paul M. Angle, ed., *Created Equal? The Complete Lincoln-Douglas Debates of 1858* (Chicago, 1958), p. 117.

4. Ibid.

5. August 29, 1891. Quoted in John R. Bovee, introduction to Ignatius Donnelly, *Doctor Huguet* (New York, 1969), pp. vi–vii.

6. Ibid., p. iv.

7. From the Donnelly Mss., Minnesota Historical Society; quoted in Ridge, p. 295.

8. Ibid., p. 296.

9. Ibid., p. 301.

10. Ignatius Donnelly, *The Golden Bottle or The Story of Ephraim Benezet of Kansas* (St. Paul, 1892), p. 3. Further page references to this work are provided in the text.

11. Diary entry, November 3, 1892, from the Donnelly Mss., Minnesota Historical Society; quoted in Ridge, p. 308.

Chapter Six

1. Ignatius Donnelly, *The American People's Money* (Chicago, 1895); quoted in Ridge, p. 346.

2. *The American People's Money*, pp. 12–15. Further page references to this work are provided in the text.

3. *The Cipher in the Plays and on the Tombstone*, Preface, n.p.
4. *St. Paul Representative*, September 13, 1893; quoted in Ridge, p. 324.
5. Ibid., November 15, 1893; quoted in Ridge, p. 325.
6. Ibid., September 20, 1893; quoted in Ridge, p. 325.
7. Ibid., November 8, 1893; quoted in Ridge, p. 325.
8. *Minneapolis Representative*, September 12, 1894; quoted in Ridge, p. 337.
9. Ibid., May 9, 1894; quoted in Ridge, p. 332.
10. Ibid., June 1, 1898; quoted in Ridge, p. 382.
11. *St. Paul Representative*, March 28, 1894; quoted in Ridge, p. 329.
12. *Minneapolis Representative*, July 4, 1894; quoted in Ridge, p. 334.
13. Ibid., November 7, 1894; quoted in Ridge, p. 339.
14. Ibid., November 4, 1896; quoted in Ridge, p. 365.
15. Quoted in Ridge, p. 399.

Selected Bibliography

PRIMARY SOURCES

1. Books

The American People's Money. Chicago: Laird & Lee, 1895. Reprinted: Westport, Conn.: Hyperion Press, 1976.
Atlantis: The Antediluvian World. New York: Harper & Bros., 1882. Reprinted: New York: Gramercy Press, 1949 (ed. Egerton Sykes).
Caesar's Column. Chicago: Free Speech Publishers, 1890. Reprinted: Cambridge: Harvard University Press, 1960 (ed. Walter Rideout).
The Cipher in the Plays and on the Tombstone. Minneapolis: Veralam Publishing Co., 1899.
Doctor Huguet. Chicago: F. J. Schulte & Co., 1891. Reprinted: New York: Arno Press, 1969.
The Golden Bottle or the Story of Ephraim Benezet of Kansas. St. Paul: D. D. Merrill Co., 1892.
The Great Cryptogram. Chicago: R. S. Peale & Co., 1887.
Ragnarok: The Age of Fire and Gravel. New York: D. Appleton & Co., 1883.

2. Pamphlets, Journal Publications, and Private Printings

An Address of the Anti Monopoly Party of Minnesota to their Constituents. Privately printed, 1874.
Address to the Republican Committee of the Second Congressional District. Privately printed, 1868.
Facts for the Granges. Privately printed, 1873.
"The Forest Fountain," *Graham's Magazine* (April 1852), reprinted in Alexander N. DeMenil, *The Literature of the Louisiana Territory.* St. Louis, 1904.
Freedman's Bureau. Privately printed, 1866.
Homestead Law. Privately printed, 1868.
In Memoriam. Privately printed, 1895.
Minnesota. New York: Folger & Turner, 1857.
The Mourner's Vision. Philadelphia: King & Baird, 1850.
A Tribute to Abraham Lincoln. Privately printed, 1865. Reprinted, Washington, D.C., 1942.
The Unjust Tariff. 1870.
Preamble to National People's Party Platform of 1892, in George B. Tindall, ed., *A Populist Reader* (New York: Harper & Row, 1966).

3. Articles

"Delia Bacon's Unhappy Story," *North American Review* 148 (March 1889).
"The Shakespeare Myth," *North American Review* 145 (June 1887).

4. Collections of Papers

The Donnelly Papers, The Minnesota Historical Society, St. Paul, Minnesota. The most complete, including mss. of books and articles.
The Donnelly Papers, The Widener Library, Harvard University, Cambridge, Massachusetts.
Other important papers are held in the following libraries:
    Chicago Historical Society, Chicago, Illinois.
    Columbia University, New York.
    Cornell University, Ithaca, New York.
    New York Public Library, New York.
    Yale University, New Haven, Connecticut.

SECONDARY SOURCES

ANDERSON, DAVID D. "Minnesota's Seven-Storied Mountaineer," *Midwestern Miscellany II* (1975). A sympathetic overview.
ANGLE, PAUL M., ed. *Created Equal? The Complete Lincoln-Douglas Debates of 1858.* Chicago: University of Chicago Press, 1958. Contains Lincoln's view of race and equality.
AXELROD, ALLAN M. "Ideology and Utopia in the Works of Ignatius Donnelly," *American Studies* 12 (Fall 1971). A sympathetic overview.
BLACK, HUGO. "Fra Ba Wrt Ear Ay," *North American Review* 145 (October 1887). Supports Donnelly; suggests a cypher in Shakespeare's epitaph.
BOVEE, JOHN R. "Doctor Huguet: Donnelly on Being Black," *Minnesota History* 41 (Summer 1969). A good discussion of the novel and Donnelly's sympathy.
DEMENIL, ALEXANDER N. *The Literature of the Louisiana Territory.* St. Louis: St. Louis News Company, 1904. Reprints Donnelly's "The Forest Fountain."
DEMEULES, DONALD H. "Ignatius Donnelly: A Don Quixote in the World of Science," *Minnesota History* 36 (June 1961). Comments on Donnelly's lack of scientific training and eagerness to draw scientific conclusions.
FISH, EVERETT W. *Donnelliana: An Appendix to Caesar's Column.* Chicago: F. J. Schulte & Co., 1892. A typical campaign biography.
FLANAGAN, JOHN T. "Letter from Holmes to Donnelly," *American Literature* 13 (March 1941). Prints and comments on Oliver Wendell Holmes's letter of July 30, 1849.
FRIEDMAN, WILLIAM F. and ELIZABETH S. *The Shakespeare Cyphers Examined.* Cambridge, Eng.: Cambridge University Press, 1957. Concludes Donnelly's system is invalid.
HANDLIN, OSCAR. "American Views of the Jew at the Opening of the

Twentieth Century," *Publications of the American Jewish Historical Society* 40 (June 1951). First major assertion of anti-Semitism in Populism, citing Donnelly as a major influence.

HART, JAMES D. *The Popular Book: A History of America's Literary Taste.* New York: Oxford University Press, 1950. Comments on *Caesar's Column* as second only to *Looking Backward* in popularity of utopian novels.

HINGHAM, JOHN. "Anti-Semitism in the Gilded Age: a Reinterpretation," *Mississippi Valley Historical Review* 43 (March 1957). Challenges Handlin; sees Donnelly's view of the Jew as sympathetic and ambivalent.

HOFSTADER, RICHARD. *The Age of Reform: From Bryan to F.D.R.* New York: Alfred Knopf, 1955. Sees *Caesar's Column* as sadistic, antiutopian, cynical, typical of a conspiratorial concept of history.

JAHER, FREDERICK C. *Doubters and Dissenters: Cataclysmic Thought in America, 1883-1915.* New York: Free Press, 1964. Sees Donnelly as fusion of radicalism and reaction and essentially tragic.

KAHN, DAVID. *The Codebreakers.* New York: Macmillan & Co., 1967. Says Donnelly "overcryptanalyzes," resulting in invalid solutions.

NICHOLSON, ALDWELL. *No Cipher in Shakespeare.* London: T. F. Unwin, 1888. Refutes Baconian cypher theories.

PATTERSON, JOHN S. "Alliance and Antipathy: Ignatius Donnelly's Ambivalent Vision in *Doctor Huguet*," *American Quarterly* 22 (Winter 1970). Emphasizes Donnelly's sympathy toward blacks and hatred to injustice, but points out Donnelly's revulsion toward blackness.

―――. "From Yeoman to Beast: Images of Blackness in *Caesar's Column*," *American Studies* 12 (Fall 1971). Cites relationship between racial imagery and violence but denies that it is associated with such images in the fiction of Thomas Dixon and others.

POLLACK, NORMAN. "Handlin on Anti-Semitism: A Critique of American Views of the Jews," *Journal of American History* 51 (December 1964). Refutes Handlin's interpretation of *Caesar's Column* as "oversimplified and misinterpreted."

―――. "Ignatius Donnelly on Human Rights: A Study of Two Novels," *Mid-America* 47 (April 1965). Defines Donnelly's position sympathetically; uses *The Golden Bottle* and *Doctor Huguet* to refute Handlin.

―――. "The Myth of Populist Anti-Semitism," *American Historical Review* 68 (October 1962). Sees Populism as ambivalent, tolerant, sympathetic.

―――, ed. *The Populist Mind.* Indianapolis and New York: Bobbs-Merrill Co., 1967. In introduction, defends Donnelly on civil and human rights.

RIDGE, MARTIN. "The Humor of Ignatius Donnelly," *Minnesota History* 33 (Autumn 1953). Sees Donnelly as humorist and wit, especially in use of dialect stories.

―――. *Ignatius Donnelly: Portrait of a Politician.* Chicago: University of Chicago Press, 1962. The definitive study of Donnelly's political career and ideas.

SAXTON, ALEXANDER. "Caesar's Column: The Dialogue of Utopia and

Catastrophe," *American Quarterly* 19 (Summer 1967). Describes the novel as "a powerful projection of catastrophe."

VINTON, ARTHUR D. "Those Wonderful Ciphers," *North American Review* 145 (November 1887). Attacks Donnelly's discovery of the cypher in the plays.

ZIFF, LARZER. *The American 1890s: Life and Times of a Lost Generation.* New York: Viking Press, 1966. Offers an interesting discussion of Donnelly as an example of the nineteenth-century "Midwestern Imagination": simple, clear, practical, romantic.

Index